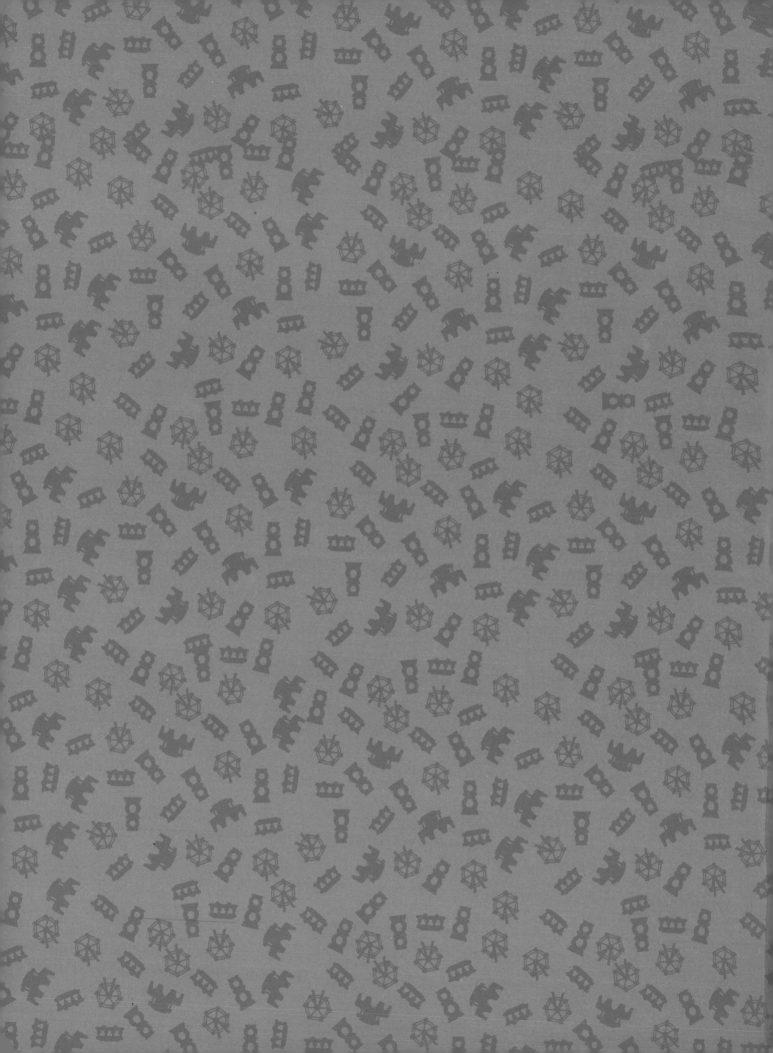

Let's Play Together!

Table of Contents

Arts & Crafts   14

Games 66

Building Blocks 110

Growing Up 160

Feelings & Imagination 184

Playing Together 224

Cooking Together 254

Daniel Tiger's Favorite Songs 276

Find a way to play together!

The Importance of Creative Play

For a child, playing isn't just a way to have fun. In fact, when children play, they're working—working on developing new abilities, understanding math and science concepts, building social skills and even expressing their feelings.

Each one of the 365 activities in this book is designed to help your child grow on the inside just as much as they're growing on the outside each day. As Mister Rogers knew, creating art, playing games and pretending are the best ways children can learn about the world and their place in it.

 # Won't You Be My Neighbor?

It's a beautiful day in the neighborhood
A beautiful day for a neighbor
Would you be mine?
Could you be mine?
Won't you be my neighbor?

It's Daniel Tiger's Neighborhood
A land of make-believe
Won't you ride along with me
It's Daniel Tiger's Neighborhood
So much to do, so much to see
Won't you ride along with me

I've got lots of friends for you to meet
In this land of make-believe
A friendly face on every street
Just waiting to greet you

Prince Wednesday skips royally by
Miss Elaina's waving hi
Won't you ride along with me

O the Owl's reading a book
Katerina's twirling, look
Won't you ride along with me

It's a beautiful day in the neighborhood
A beautiful day for a neighbor
In Daniel Tiger's Neighborhood

See more song lyrics from Daniel Tiger's Neighborhood on page 276.

11

Tutorials

Make your own arts and crafts supplies.

Homemade Modeling Dough

- 2 cups flour
- 1 cup salt
- 1 cup water
- 1 tsp vegetable oil

Combine all ingredients and store in an airtight container.

Self-Hardening Modeling Dough

- 1½ cups salt
- 4 cups flour
- 1½ cups water

Mix all ingredients together and knead. Creations made from this mixture should harden overnight. Baking and/or painting final products will hinder mold.

Homemade Fingerpaint

- 1 cup mild soap flakes or soap powder
- ½ cup water
- Food coloring or paint

Whip the soap and water until thick and frothy with a wire whisk or hand mixer. Add a few drops of food coloring or a little bit of paint to make your desired color.

Homemade Glue

- 1 cup flour
- 1 cup cold water
- 3 cups boiling water

Mix flour and cold water in a mixing bowl. Add this mixture to 3 cups boiling water and cook for about 10 minutes. Store in an airtight container. The paste will keep for several days.

If there's something you need, try to make it yourself!

Arts & Crafts

Express creativity through painting, drawing, coloring and more.

Painting Boxes

Help your child learn how to develop creative play.

You'll Need

- Boxes of various sizes
- Nontoxic paint and brushes, or fingerpaint
- Aprons or paint shirts
- Newspaper or an old tablecloth

Directions

1. Let your child choose one or more boxes to paint. Have your child help you cover a work area with newspaper.

2. Let your child decide which colors or designs to put on their box.

3. Get painting!

Things to Talk About

- With a little imagination, a box can be anything! What should you turn your box into?

If it's nice out, you can do this activity outside!

Cardboard Trumpets

Help your child learn how to express their feelings through music.

You'll Need

- Cardboard paper towel rolls
- Markers or crayons
- Glue
- Aluminum foil (optional)
- Buttons (optional)

Directions

1. First, if desired, cover the paper towel rolls with aluminum foil to make shiny "metal" trumpets.

2. Help your child draw or glue buttons on the tubes to make pretend finger holes.

3. Show your child how to hum through the tube to make a kazoo-like sound.

Try "playing" a song that you both know together!

Things to Talk About

- Can you make happy music?
- What does sad music sound like?
- What does lonely music sound like?

String Paintings

Help your child develop their imagination.

You'll Need

- Nontoxic paint
- Paper
- String (foot-long pieces)
- Crayons or markers
- Newspapers

Directions

1. Cover the play area with plenty of newspaper.

2. Let your child dip a piece of string in the paint. Have them place the string on a piece of paper, leaving part of the string sticking out.

3. Fold the paper and press down, then pull out the string. Once the paint has dried, let your child add to the design with crayons or markers.

Things to Talk About

- Do the designs make you think of anything?
- What do they look like?

Inside Oranges

Help your child learn about food and the world.

You'll Need

- Orange
- Large piece of paper
- Orange paint and brushes, or orange crayons
- Glue
- Several 3-inch circles cut from paper

Directions

1. Peel an orange for your child. Ask them questions about it. Are there any seeds? How does it taste, smell and feel? Where do oranges come from?

2. Help your child make an orange tree. Draw a trunk and branches on the large piece of paper. Let your child color or paint the circles orange and help them glue the circles to the tree. Add green leaves, if you'd like.

Things to Talk About

- Is the peel thick or thin?
- What shape are oranges?
- Can you name other fruits with the same shape?

You can recreate this activity with other fruits too!

Paper Plate Masks

Help your child try out different roles.

You'll Need

- Paper plates
- Markers or crayons
- Scrap materials (yarn, buttons, paper, cloth, etc)
- Glue
- Ice pop sticks
- Tape

Directions

1. Have younger children draw faces on the paper plates, while older children may use scrap materials to glue faces onto their masks, like yarn hair and button eyes.

2. Help your child tape a ice pop stick to the back of the mask so it can be held up.

3. Let your child play with the mask or use it as a puppet.

You can also make eye holes for the masks.

Things to Talk About

- Show young children how easily the mask can be taken away. Talk about how the person behind the mask is still the person they know.

Tissue Paper Pictures

Help your child recognize likeness and difference, and understand and accept individual differences.

You'll Need

- Tissue paper in several colors
- Tray or shoebox
- Diluted glue
- Cotton swabs or small brushes
- Background paper

Directions

1. Have your child tear the tissue paper into small pieces, placing the scraps in a tray or shoebox.

2. Let your child use the cotton swab to paint a piece of background paper with the diluted glue, then arrange the tissue scraps on the sticky surface. If only one child is doing the project, make one yourself too!

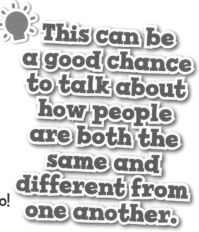

This can be a good chance to talk about how people are both the same and different from one another.

Things to Talk About

- How are the pictures similar?
- How are they different?

Making a Book

Help your child develop their imagination and practice making choices.

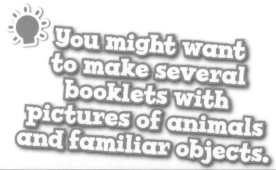

You'll Need

- Thin cardboard
  (like from a cereal box)
- Paper for pages
  (heavy paper works best)
- Scraps of material
- Glue
- Yarn, shoelaces or heavy string
- Old magazines or catalogs

Directions

1. Make the front and back covers for your child's book by cutting pieces of cardboard a little larger than the pages you'll be using. Let your child glue scraps of material on the cardboard to make a fancy cover.

2. Place five or six pieces of paper between the covers, poke holes along the sides and lace the booklets together with yarn.

3. Let your child fill the book with anything that interests them. They can cut out images from old magazines, write a short story or draw something.

Things to Talk About

- Would your child like to make up a poem or song to write in the book?
- What do they like about their books?

You might want to make several booklets with pictures of animals and familiar objects.

Handprint Cards

Help your child express their feelings through artwork and practice working together.

You'll Need

- One sheet of folded paper for each child
- Nontoxic paint
- Brush
- Soap and water

Directions

1. Give your child a folded piece of paper. Paint a thin coat of paint on the inside of their hand. Let them choose where to put the handprint on their card.

2. Once the card is dry, have your child write their name on the card (or just mark it if they can't write their name yet).

Things to Talk About

- What would your child like the card to say?
- Do they want to give it to someone special?

Paper Cup Containers

Help your child develop creative play and learn about differences.

You'll Need

- Paper cups
- Yarn
- Felt scraps
- Tissue paper
- Markers
- Liquid glue
- Cotton swabs or small brushes

Directions

1. Give your child a cup and let them decorate it however they like. They can use markers, glue on tissue paper or felt, or wrap the cup with yarn.

2. If you are doing this activity with just one child, decorate a cup for yourself too.

3. Once the cups are finished, ask your child what they would like to do with the cup. It could hold crayons, change or be a gift.

Things to Talk About

- Why do your cups look different?
- Talk about how different people make different cups because each person is different.

Decorating is easier if you turn the cup upside down first.

Stick Designs

Help your child develop their imagination.

You'll Need

- Popsicle sticks or 1½-inch-wide strips of construction paper

- Thin cardboard (like insides of cereal boxes)

- Diluted glue (mix one part water to one part glue)

Directions

1. Spread out all the supplies on a table and let your child play with them.

2. Help your child glue the sticks to the cardboard to make a design of their choosing.

Things to Talk About

- What kinds of things can you make from the sticks?
- Can you make letters? Outlines of buildings or trees? Your name?

Keep leftover supplies in a special box that your child can play with whenever they like.

An Old Shoebox

Help your child learn about being resourceful.

You'll Need

- Empty shoebox
- Scraps of paper or cloth
- Yarn
- Glue
- Crayons or markers

Talk about how the same materials can make lots of different things.

Directions

1. Show your child the supplies and ask them what they could make out of the shoebox.

2. Help your child decorate the shoebox to turn it into something new.

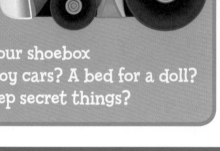

Things to Talk About

- What do you want your shoebox to be? A garage for toy cars? A bed for a doll? A special place to keep secret things?

Paper Windows

Help your child develop their memory.

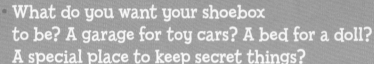

You'll Need

- Two pieces of paper
- Crayons or markers
- Tape
- Scissors

Directions

1. Give your child a piece of paper and have them make "windows" by drawing squares on the paper. Using scissors, cut around three sides of each box and have your child fold it back to create a flap.

2. Tape this paper on top of a second piece of paper and open the "windows." Have your child draw pictures inside each window.

3. Once finished, your child can play a peekaboo game by opening and closing the windows.

You can make the windows open in any direction!

Things to Talk About

- Can you remember which picture is behind which window?

Stone Paperweights

Help your child practice their artistic skills.

You'll Need

- An assortment of stones
- Pan of water
- Paper towels
- Nontoxic paint
- Brushes
- Liquid glue
- Paper or cloth scraps, cotton, yarn, etc
- Newspaper

Directions

1. Rinse the stones and have your child dry them with paper towels.

2. Cover your work area with newspaper.

3. Encourage your child to decorate their stone any way they'd like.

Things to Talk About

- What can you make your stone look like?
- How would you add eyes or whiskers?

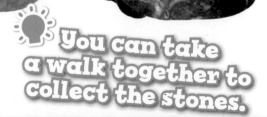

You can take a walk together to collect the stones.

Flying Ghosts

Help your child understand the difference between real and pretend, and use play to learn about feelings.

You'll Need

- White tissues
- Thread or dental floss
- Felt-tipped marker
- Cotton balls (optional)

Directions

1. Help your child make a "ghost" by wrapping a tissue around a few cotton balls or another crumpled tissue. Gather the tissue to make a neck and tie it with thread or dental floss. Leave a long piece of thread so your child can make their ghost "fly."

2. If you like, give your ghost a face with a felt-tipped marker.

3. Let your child make the ghost "fly."

Things to Talk About

- Are ghosts real or pretend?
- Is your ghost moving by itself or does it need someone to make it move?

This is a good activity for when your child is feeling afraid.

My Family and Me

Help your child work on feelings about separation and express their feelings through artwork.

You'll Need

- Pictures of your family (photos or drawings)
- Paper
- Glue
- Crayons or markers
- Stapler

Directions

1. Help your child paste or draw pictures of your family members on separate pieces of paper. Make sure to include a picture of your child too!

2. Help your child label the pictures with everyone's names.

3. Staple all of the pages together to make a *My Family and Me* book.

Things to Talk About

- What do your family members look like?
- Do you know all of their names?
- What are some things you like to do with your family?

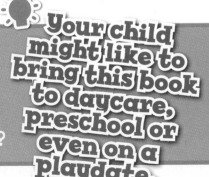

Your child might like to bring this book to daycare, preschool or even on a playdate.

Camouflage

Help your child learn more about the world.

You'll Need

- Colored paper
- White paper
- Scissors
- Glue

Directions

1. Have your child draw an animal on a white piece of paper. Help them cut it out and glue it on a piece of colored paper. Ask your child how easy it is to see their animal.

2. Give your child a second piece of colored paper and have them tear it into small pieces. Glue these pieces to the white animal, like putting spots on a leopard. Ask if it's harder to see the animal now.

If you'd like, add small pieces of white paper to the colored paper as well.

Things to Talk About

- Is it harder to see the animal when it has spots that match its surroundings? There's a word for this: camouflage.

Shoebox Trolley

Help your child develop their imagination.

You'll Need

- Empty shoebox
- Crayons or markers
- Construction paper
- Glue
- Scissors

Directions

1. Help your child cut the construction paper into a few different shapes: squares for windows, a rectangle for the front window and circles for headlights and wheels.

2. Set out the shapes and glue and help your child make a trolley or bus with the empty shoebox.

 **Make sure the glue is dry before playing with the trolley.**

Things to Talk About

- What do people use trolleys for?
- What can you use this trolley for?
- Do you have any toys that can be make-believe passengers on the trolley?

Invisible Pictures

Help your child develop their curiosity.

You'll Need

- Bar of white soap
- White paper
- Soft lead pencils
- Knife

Directions

1. Cut the bar of soap into about 1½-inch-wide strips so your child can use one like a crayon.

2. Ask your child to draw "invisible" pictures on the piece of paper. Simple letters, shapes or faces are a good place to start.

3. Show your child how to rub the side of a pencil (not the point) over the drawing to make it appear.

 **White crayons can be used in place of soap.**

Things to Talk About

- Why couldn't you see the picture at first?
- Do you want to make an invisible picture for someone?

Connect-the-Dot Designs

Help your child develop creative play.

You'll Need

- Pencils
- Paper
- Crayons and markers

Directions

1. Draw a bunch of dots on a few pieces of paper. Your child may want to help with this.

2. Let your child connect the dots with a pencil in any pattern they want. Then they can fill in the patterns with crayons or markers.

This is a good activity to do with a group of children. Let them compare their pictures and designs and talk about why they are different.

Things to Talk About

- Can you connect the dots to make different kinds of objects?

There's No One Just Like You

Help your child understand and accept individual differences.

You'll Need

- Plain paper
- Stamp pad (or paper towels, shallow dish and nontoxic paint)

Directions

1. Using a stamp pad, let your child make thumbprints and fingerprints on a piece of paper. If you don't have a stamp pad, you can make one by layering several paper towels in a shallow dish and pouring a little paint on top.

2. Make some fingerprints of your own, too, and let your child compare the prints.

Things to Talk About

- Are the prints exactly alike?
- Can you see any differences?
- What about the prints are the same?

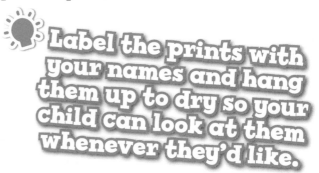 **Label the prints with your names and hang them up to dry so your child can look at them whenever they'd like.**

Leaf Rubbings

Help your child learn to look carefully and recognize likeness and difference.

You'll Need

- Different kinds of leaves
- Lightweight paper
- Crayons

Directions

1. Take your child for a walk to collect a few different kinds of leaves.

2. Place a leaf under a piece of paper and show your child how to rub a crayon across it to see the outline.

Things to Talk About

- How are the leaves alike and different from one another?
- How are the rubbings similar to the leaves and how are they different?

 You can make rubbings from other objects too.

Purple Paint

Help your child develop their imagination and appreciate individual differences.

You'll Need

- Red paint
- Blue paint
- Paintbrushes
- Paper
- Plastic tubs (like old yogurt containers)
- Spoons

Directions

1. Ask your child if they know what the color purple is. Can they show you anything that's purple in the room?

2. Put a spoonful each of red paint and blue paint in the plastic tub. Let your child mix them together to make purple paint.

3. Let your child paint a picture using the purple paint.

You can also do this with green (by mixing blue and yellow paints) or orange (by mixing yellow and red).

Things to Talk About

- What if everything was purple?
- Would everything look the same?
- Would it be fun to be the same as everyone else all the time?

Snow Pictures

Help your child develop their creativity.

You'll Need

- Colored construction paper
- Cotton balls
- Liquid glue
- Crayons or markers

Directions

1. Have your child draw a picture of your house on a piece of paper.

2. Give your child four to five cotton balls to pull apart. Once they are in small pieces, show them how to glue the pieces to the paper to cover it in "snow."

 If it doesn't snow where you live, this is a good time to talk about different parts of the world.

Things to Talk About

- Can you still see the house covered in snow?
- Have you ever played in the snow before?
- What was it like?

Make a Piñata

Help your child practice both working cooperatively and waiting.

You'll Need

- Large balloon
- Strips of newspaper (1-by-12-inches)
- Diluted paste or glue
- Dishpan

Things to Talk About

- Do you know what a piñata is?
- Was it difficult to wait for it to be dry?
- What would have happened if you didn't wait?

Directions

1. Blow up a balloon and tie it closed. Soak newspaper strips in a dishpan of diluted glue. Cover the balloon with the strips, making five or six layers.

2. Let the balloon dry for several days. Once it's dry, you can decorate it if you like.

3. Cut a small hole in the piñata, popping the balloon inside. It can now be filled with small toys or nutritious snacks.

Nighttime Pictures

Help your child learn more about their world and develop their imagination.

You'll Need

- Paper
- Star shapes cut from construction paper
- Moon cut out from construction paper
- Glue
- Black or gray construction paper
- Crayons, markers or white chalk

Directions

1. Ask your child to paste one moon and many star shapes anywhere they'd like on the dark construction paper.

2. Let your child try to draw on the paper with the markers. When they can't see it very well, show them how they can draw with the white chalk.

Things to Talk About

- It's very difficult to see at night. What does the sky look like at night?
- Does the moon always look the same?

You might want to find a library book or look up a children's website to help talk to your child about stars and the moon.

My Special Box

Help your child learn more about privacy.

You'll Need

- Shoebox with cover
- Scrap materials, like felt or colored paper
- Glue
- Markers or crayons

Directions

1. Give your child a shoebox and let them decorate it with the materials you've put out.

2. Help your child write their name on the box. Ask them if they have any special toys or items they would like to keep in the box. They don't have to share these things with anyone else.

Things to Talk About

- Talk about how it's good to share, but everyone is allowed to have things they keep private too.
- It's important to not touch other people's things when they don't want you to.

Making Pillows

Help your child learn how things are made.

You'll Need

- Fabric
- Markers
- Needle and thread, or sewing machine
- Stuffing (store-bought or cotton balls)

Directions

1. Cut out two pieces of fabric for either side of the pillow. They can be any size or shape you like, but small rectangles or squares are easy to work with.

2. Let your child draw on the fabric if they'd like, or help them write their name on it.

3. Sew the pieces of fabric together, leaving one end open. Have your child help you stuff the pillow with filling. Finish sewing the pillow closed.

Things to Talk About

- What is the pillow made of?
- Can you tell what's inside the pillow?
- What else could you fill a pillow with?
- What wouldn't be good to fill a pillow with?

You will have to do the sewing, but your child might like to watch.

Body Outlines

Help your child understand the difference between real and pretend.

You'll Need

- Large sheets of paper (or the insides of paper grocery bags taped together)
- Markers or crayons

Directions

1. Have your child lay down on the pieces of paper and trace the outline of their body on the paper.

2. Let your child draw in their own face and clothing.

3. Cut out the outline and hang it up.

Things to Talk About

- How is your outline like you?
- How is it different?

You may want to remind your child that statues and pictures are not real people, they are just made to show what that person looks like.

Yarn Designs

Help your child develop muscle control and the ability to keep trying.

You'll Need

- Thin cardboard, like from a cereal box
- Yarn
- Tape
- Sharp pencil or hole punch

Directions

1. Using a hole punch or sharp pencil, make an assortment of holes in the cardboard.

2. Wrap tape around one end of the yarn to make a hard tip that will thread easily.

3. Show your child how to thread the yarn through the holes to make different patterns.

Your child may like doing this with different colors of yarn.

Things to Talk About

- Are there different patterns you can make?
- Does trying something new get easier the more you do it?

Sparkle Paintings

Help your child express their creativity.

When the paint dries, the salt will glisten.

You'll Need

- Flour
- Salt
- Water
- Food coloring (optional)
- Containers
- Brushes
- Cardboard or heavy paper

Directions

1. Mix equal parts of flour, salt and water to create a "sparkle" paint. Food coloring can be added to make the paint a different color.

2. Let your child paint a picture with the sparkle paint.

Things to Talk About

- What does "sparkle" mean?
- Can you think of some things that sparkle?
- What is happening in your sparkle painting?

Fabric Cards

Help your child feel proud of their accomplishments.

You'll Need

- Scraps of fabric
- Yarn, ribbon or lace
- Glue
- Heavy paper folded to make a card

Directions

1. Let your child decorate the front of the card with the fabric pieces.

2. Ask your child to pick someone to give the card to and come up with a message to write inside.

Things to Talk About

- How does it feel to make something special?
- Do you like giving gifts to people you love?

Use fabrics with different colors, textures and patterns.

Paper Bag Puppets

Help your child develop creative play.

You'll Need

- Paper bags (like brown lunch bags)
- Scrap materials (like yarn, paper, fabric, buttons, etc.)
- Glue
- Crayons or markers
- Tape

Directions

1. Show your child how a paper bag can be made into a puppet, making eyes and a nose on the base and moving it up and down to make a "mouth."

2. Let your child create their own puppet with the materials you've gathered.

3. Use the puppets to act out a pretend scene.

Things to Talk About

- What about the puppets is the same?
- What is different?
- Do you want to give each puppet a name?

Paint Blots

Help your child develop artistic skills.

This is a good group activity.

You'll Need

- Nontoxic paint
- Paper
- Crayons or markers

Directions

1. Give your child a piece of paper and help them fold it in half. Open the paper and put a small blob of paint on one side.

2. Have your child close the paper again and rub it around. Unfold the paper. What does your blot look like?

3. Once the paint dries, have your child draw more details around their blot.

Things to Talk About

- What else could the blot be?
- What if you turn it upside down?

Bookmarks

Help your child develop their imagination and learn more about the world.

You'll Need

- Cardboard or heavy paper, cut into 2-by-5-inch strips
- Crayons, paint or markers
- Fabric scraps, yarn, etc.
- Glue
- Clear nail polish

Directions

1. Explain how bookmarks help us save our place in books.

2. Let your child to color or paint their bookmark any way they'd like, or glue small pieces of fabric to it.

Things to Talk About

- What is your favorite book?
- Do you have a favorite part you would like to mark?

Apply a coat of clear nail polish to seal in the colors on the bookmarks so they don't rub off on any books.

Sock Puppets

Help your child express their feelings.

You'll Need

- Socks
- Scrap materials, like buttons, paper, fabric, yarn, etc.
- Glue
- Needle and thread (optional)

Directions

1. Show your child how to slip the sock over their hand and use it to make a puppet.

2. Using the scrap materials, help your child sew or glue on eyes, a nose, hair or anything else they'd like.

3. If something has been bothering your child, they might want to act it out with the puppets.

Things to Talk About

- Do you feel better when you talk about your feelings?
- Would you like to use the puppet next time you're feeling upset?

This is a good activity if your child has been feeling scared or upset.

Homemade Marionettes

Help your child develop storytelling skills.

You'll Need

- Stuffed animal
- String
- Ruler or paper towel tube
- Real puppet, if you have one

Things to Talk About

- Do you know what a marionette is?
- Do you want to tell a story with it?

You can make multiple marionettes and put on a play.

Directions

1. Use a real puppet or look up a video to show your child how they work.

2. Tie strings to the head, arms and legs of your stuffed animal and attach the other ends to a ruler or paper towel tube to make your own marionette.

3. Let your child play with the marionette and make it move on their own.

39

Finger Painting Designs

Help your child develop their creativity.

You'll Need

- Glossy contact paper cut into foot-long strips
- Water
- Sponge
- Finger paint
- Newspaper or plastic
- Old shirts or aprons

Directions

1. Let your child sponge down the glossy side of the paper with water.

2. Have your child use the finger paints to make their own designs on the contact paper.

Things to Talk About

- Can you use your palms to paint?
- What about your knuckles or the sides of your hands?

This activity can be messy—do it outside or cover your workspace with newspaper.

Crayon Window Hangings

Help your child develop artistic skills.

You'll Need

- Old crayon pieces
- Crayon sharpener or plastic knife
- Wax paper
- Iron

Directions

1. Shave off small pieces of crayon onto a piece of wax paper. Have your child place another piece of wax paper over this one.

2. Gently press the sheets together with a warm iron.

You can hang this in a window to let light shine through, like stained glass.

Things to Talk About

- Do you think you could make this exact same pattern again?
- Do you want to try this again and make a special design?

Paper Plate Shakers

Help your child learn to listen carefully.

You'll Need

- Two paper plates
- Beads
- Stapler or tape
- Crayons or markers

Directions

1. Use a stapler or tape to fasten the two plates together, leaving a small gap. Let your child add some beads to the shaker, then finish sealing it.

2. Have your child decorate the shaker any way they'd like then use it to make their own music.

Things to Talk About

- Do you want to use the shaker while singing?
- Do you know what a tambourine is?

Clay Sculptures

Help your child develop creative play.

You'll Need

- Clay or modeling dough (see recipe on page 12)
- Cookie-cutters, Popsicle sticks, rolling pin or other "tools"

Directions

1. If you don't have any clay on hand, use the recipe on page 12 to make some.

2. Let your child play with the clay. Older children might like to try to make animals, while younger children can use cookie-cutters or make balls, "pancakes" or "cookies."

Things to Talk About

- How does the clay feel?
- What kinds of things can you make out of clay?

You can let the sculptures harden overnight then paint them the next day.

Torn Paper Pictures

Help your child develop both muscle control and their creativity.

You'll Need

- Easy-to-tear, brightly colored paper (newspaper, tissue paper, etc.)
- Glue
- Water
- Small bowl
- Brush
- Heavier background paper

Directions

1. Put one part glue and one part water in the bowl and mix to combine.

2. Meanwhile, have your child tear up the bright paper into small pieces.

3. Let your child create their own collage by first spreading the glue on the paper and adding the torn paper as they choose.

Glitter, cut-out pictures and cut-up ribbon are good additions to this activity.

Things to Talk About

- Do you know what a collage is?
- Next time, what else would you add to your collage?

Dinosaur Models

Help your child develop their imagination and learn more about the world around them.

You'll Need

- Clay or modeling dough (recipe on page 12)
- Paper
- Crayons or markers
- Dinosaur book, or print-outs from an educational website

Directions

1. Ask your child what they know about dinosaurs. What did they look like? Are they still around today?

2. Show your child the information about dinosaurs.

3. Let your child sculpt their own dinosaur from the clay.

Things to Talk About

- Are these real dinosaurs?
- How do we know what dinosaurs looked like?

You can also have your child draw pictures of dinosaurs and show them different kinds.

Ways to Say "I Love You"

Help your child talk about feelings and understand and accept individual differences.

You may want to sing "Find Your Own Way To Say I Love You" on page 281.

You'll Need

- Scissors
- Paper
- Stapler
- Crayons or markers

Directions

1. Ask your child how they know their parents and family members love them. What do they do to show their love?

2. Can your child think of things they do to show they love somebody?

3. Fold a few sheets of paper in half and staple them together at the "spine" to make a booklet. Let your child draw pictures of the different ways people show love on each page.

Things to Talk About

- Do you tell people you love them?
- Do hugs show love?
- What about preparing meals, helping clean or giving gifts?

An Art Show

Help your child feel proud of their accomplishments.

You'll Need

- Paper
- Crayons or markers
- Nontoxic paint
- Brushes
- Glue
- Scrap paper

Directions

1. Have your child choose what kind of art they would like to make: a drawing, painting or collage.

2. Let your child make their piece of art. Make your own art too!

3. Hang up the finished pieces and label them with your names. Take time to admire what you both have created.

Things to Talk About

- Do you know what a gallery is?
- Do you like looking at art?

A Rainbow for Everyone

Help your child practice working together and learn more about the world around them.

You'll Need

- Paper grocery bag
- Crayons or colored markers

Directions

1. Cut open the grocery bag. Use a marker to draw the outline of a rainbow on the inside of the flattened grocery bag.

2. Mark each section with the proper color: red, orange, yellow, green, blue, indigo, violet. Have your child help you color in each section.

Things to Talk About

- Do you know the colors of a rainbow?
- Have you ever seen a real rainbow?

Stuffie

Help your child practice working cooperatively.

You'll Need

- Old pillowcase
- Stuffing materials (clean old rags or clothes)
- Yarn or string
- Buttons, fabric scraps, etc
- Fabric glue, or needle and thread

Directions

1. Have your child help you fill the pillowcase. Tie the end closed with yarn or string. You might want to also tie around the middle to make a waist, or around corners to make ears or feet.

2. Have your child help you decorate the toy. Buttons, scraps of fabric and yarn could become eyes, a mouth, hair, etc.

"Stuffie" can make for a good cuddling toy.

Things to Talk About

- Do you like helping to make something new?
- Do you want to think of on a name for your new softee?

46

Animal Blocks

Help your child practice pretending.

If you make enough blocks, you can have a pretend animal parade.

You'll Need

- Pictures of animals (printed out or cut from magazines)
- Tape
- Wood blocks or small milk cartons, rinsed
- Scissors

Directions

1. Have your child help you cut out the pictures of animals and then tape one to each box.

2. Let your child play with the animal blocks and pretend they are real animals.

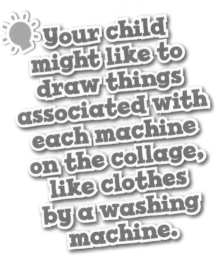

Things to Talk About

- Can you name each animal?
- Do you know what sounds they each make?

Machine Collage

Help your child learn more about the world.

Your child might like to draw things associated with each machine on the collage, like clothes by a washing machine.

You'll Need

- Magazines and catalogs
- Large piece of paper
- Glue
- Common machines (television, smartphone, small appliances, etc.)

Directions

1. Take a tour of your house and see if your child can identify some machines. Explain what each machine does and how it helps people.

2. Help your child make a machine collage by cutting out pictures from magazines or catalogs and gluing them to a large piece of paper.

Things to Talk About

- Where do machines come from?
- Why do people make machines?

Balloon Faces

Help your child express feelings through art.

You'll Need

- Blown-up balloon
- Scrap materials (paper, cloth, yarn, etc.)
- Strip of construction paper, about 2-by-8-inches
- Glue

Directions

1. Make a stand for your balloon by gluing the ends of the construction paper together.

2. Put out the scrap materials and glue and let your child make a face on the balloon.

Things to Talk About

- Is your balloon happy? Sad?
- Is it feeling funny or upset?

Remind your child that balloon faces are just pretend faces.

Coin Banks

Help your child learn more about money.

You'll Need

- Plastic tubs and lids (like from a yogurt container)
- Knife or scissors
- Glue
- Paper scraps
- Yarn
- Coins

Directions

1. Cut a slit large enough for a coin in the center of the lid. Let your child put the lid back on the container.

2. Let your child decorate the "bank" and add a few coins to it.

You might want to let your child start saving coins toward a small toy or treat.

Things to Talk About

- What do we use money for?
- What can you buy with your change?

Straws

Help your child develop their imagination.

You'll Need

- Straws
- Safety scissors
- Yarn
- Tape
- Paper
- Glue

Directions

1. Use the straws to have a drink of water, milk or juice.

2. Afterward, rinse them out and decide how they can be used for something else. Your child may want to cut up the straws and put them on a piece of yarn to make a necklace, use them to decorate a piece of paper or pretend they're pipes or drains while playing with other toys.

Things to Talk About

- What other ways can you use the straws again?
- Why is it good to use things more than once?

Aquarium Pictures

Help your child learn more about their world.

You'll Need

- Paper
- Fish shapes cut from construction paper
- Glue
- Water
- Food coloring (blue or green)
- Paper cups
- Brushes
- Markers or crayons

Directions

1. Once you have cut out a variety of fish shapes, spread them out on a table and let your child select some they would like to paste on their paper. Encourage your child to add seaweed, rocks and even other fish by drawing them in.

2. Let your child paint over the picture with a mixture of food coloring and water, making everything look "underwater."

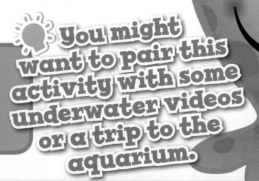

You might want to pair this activity with some underwater videos or a trip to the aquarium.

Things to Talk About

- Where do fish live?
- Have you ever seen a real fish?

Self-Portraits

Help your child learn more about their body and understand and accept individual differences.

You'll Need

- Paper
- Markers or crayons
- Mirror

Things to Talk About

- Do you know what a portrait is?
- Would everybody's portrait look the same?

Directions

1. Let your child look at their reflection in a mirror. Can they point out their eyes, nose, mouth, etc?

2. Have your child draw a self-portrait, letting them look in the mirror again while doing so, if they wish.

Animal Family Posters

Help your child recognize likeness and difference, and to understand and accept individual differences.

You'll Need

- Magazines
- Glue
- Large pieces of paper or thin cardboard
- Scissors

Directions

1. Let your child look through the magazines for pictures of animals, or print some out for them. Have your child sort animals that are the same into different piles.

2. Have your child paste groups of animals that are the same onto the piece of paper. Help your child label the different kinds of animals.

Things to Talk About

- Do you know that dogs always have puppies and cats always have kittens?
- How are you like the other people in your family?

Covered Milk Cartons

Help your child develop creative play and feel proud of their accomplishments.

You'll Need

- Empty cardboard milk carton, rinsed and dried
- Construction paper
- Tape or glue

Things to Talk About

- What else could you have turned the carton into?
- Is it fun to turn something you would have thrown out into something new?

Directions

1. Ask your child what they think they could turn the milk carton into. Maybe a house, trolley or doll bed?

2. Help your child cut the construction paper into shapes like windows, wheels, etc.

3. Have your child tape or glue the shapes on and, if necessary, help them cut out any portions of the carton to finish their design.

Younger children may just want to add pictures or pieces of paper all over the carton.

Comet Collage

Help your child express their feelings through their artwork and develop their imagination.

You'll Need

- Dark background paper
- Paper shapes to represent comets, stars, full and crescent moons, etc.
- Glue
- Glitter (optional)

Directions

1. Ask your child to picture what the sky looks like at night. Can they describe it to you?

2. Let your child sort through the paper shapes and glue them to the dark paper to make their own night sky. If you'd like, you can add tails to the comets using glitter.

Things to Talk About

- Do you know what a comet is?
- How far away do you think the stars are?

Magic Telescopes

Help your child understand the difference between real and pretend.

You'll Need

- Paper towel tubes
- Aluminum foil (optional)
- Paper or fabric
- Crayons or markers

Directions

1. Encourage your child to decorate their tube with paper or aluminum foil.

2. Have your child look through the telescope and imagine they are looking at faraway stars and planets. What else do they see?

Things to Talk About

- Are you really seeing stars, planets, rockets, etc.?
- Is it fun to pretend sometimes?

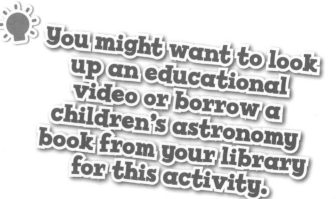

You might want to look up an educational video or borrow a children's astronomy book from your library for this activity.

Sea Collage

Help your child learn to follow directions.

Save the leftover construction paper to use as scrap material in other activities.

You'll Need

- Large rectangle of white or light blue paper
- Construction paper in various colors
- Crayons
- Watercolors
- Brushes
- Glue
- Scissors

Directions

1. Ask your child what they think it's like underwater. Using crayons, have your child draw seaweed, rocks and sea creatures on the paper.

2. Use watercolors to add darker blue or green paint to the entire picture. (The paint won't stick to crayon, so the drawings will show through.)

3. While the paint dries, cut out colorful fish shapes from the paper. Once it's dry, let your child glue them wherever they like on their underwater scene.

Things to Talk About

- Why did you use the crayon first?
- Why couldn't you glue the fish on before the paint dried?

Clothespin People

Help your child learn to use their imagination.

You'll Need

- Slotted clothespins
- Yarn
- Markers
- Fabric scraps
- Glue

Your child might like to use these toys to act out something they did recently.

Directions

1. Let your child decorate a few clothespins to look like people. They can give them yarn for hair and make clothes from fabric scraps.

2. Have your child act out a scene using the clothespin people they have just made.

Things to Talk About

- Do you want to pretend you are one of the clothespin people?
- Who else do you know that can be a clothespin person?

Dancing Feet Mobiles

Help your child learn more about body parts and understand and accept individual differences.

You'll Need

- Construction paper
- Pencil or marker
- Scissors
- Straw or hanger
- String

Directions

1. Trace around your child's foot on a piece of construction paper. Cut it out and use it as a template to cut out a few more feet.

2. Tie the feet to the straw or hanger using a piece of string. Let your child play with the mobile. Can they make the feet dance? Walk? Jump?

Things to Talk About

- What do you use your feet for?
- How do you move your feet when you're happy?

If you're doing this activity with multiple children, you can make tracings of all their feet and talk about how they're the same and different.

Star Mobiles

Help your child develop their imagination and artistic skills.

You'll Need

- Paper
- Markers
- Scissors
- String
- Clothes hanger
- Glue
- Glitter
- Pencil or hole punch

Directions

1. Have your child help you cut out star shapes or moon shapes from the paper. To make sparkling stars, drizzle liquid glue or use a glue stick to lightly coat one side of each star, then let your child sprinkle glitter on top.

2. Make holes in the shapes using a pencil or hole punch and help your child tie the stars to the hanger. Hang them at different heights to fit more on.

Young children might like to just play with a single star on a piece of string. If they spin around, they can make imaginary "shooting stars."

Things to Talk About

- What do you know about stars?
- Do you like the way they twinkle?

Paper Bag Hats

Help your child develop creative play.

You can change your hair or what you wear. But no matter what you do, you're still you!

You'll Need

- Medium-sized paper bags
- Scissors
- Glue
- Yarn
- Construction paper
- Markers
- Mirror

Directions

1. Choose a bag that fits the top of your child's head fairly snugly. Cut out the front of the bag to frame your child's face.

2. Let your child decorate their hat as they please. When finished, have your child put on the hat and look in the mirror.

Things to Talk About

- What kind of hat do you want to make?
- Do you think someone else would make a hat just like the one you did?

Recycling Projects

Help your child learn more about conservation and learn to do things independently.

You'll Need

- Assorted discarded items, such as paper towel rolls, plastic milk caps, string, ribbon, used wrapping paper, empty cardboard boxes
- Glue
- Scissors

Directions

1. Talk about the ways you can reuse or recycle boxes, paper and cardboard. Do they have any ideas?

2. Help your child turn their box into something new. Maybe they want to turn it into a toy box, a doll bed, a sculpture or a rocket ship. Or, if they have a present to give someone, they can put it in the box and decorate it.

Things to Talk About

- Why is it important to recycle?
- What does your family do to recycle things?

 Save leftover supplies for future projects or show your child where they can be recycled.

Fancy Crowns

Help your child try out different roles.

You'll Need

- Strips of construction paper or lightweight cardboard, about 4 inches wide
- Aluminum foil
- Used foil wrapping paper or metallic ribbon
- Sequins or glitter (optional)
- Scrap materials (feathers, yarn, buttons)
- Glue
- Safety scissors
- Tape

Directions

1. Measure how long the paper or cardboard need to be to make a crown on your child's head, but do not tape it together yet. It will be easier to decorate while flat.

2. Help your child cut points in the top of the crown, if they like. Let them decorate the crown with the materials you've provided.

Things to Talk About

- What kinds of people usually wear crowns?
- Do you like wearing your crown?

Paper Bag Mask

Help your child understand the difference between real and pretend.

Only use paper bags for this activity.

You'll Need

- Paper bags
- Safety scissors
- Crayons or markers
- Yarn
- Construction paper
- Glue

Directions

1. Cut off the bottom of a brown paper bag that can fit over your child's head. If you like, cut along the bottom so it rests comfortably over your child's nose.

2. Help your child cut out eye holes and then decorate their mask any way they choose. They might like to be something specific, like a cat, or just add random things to their mask.

Things to Talk About

- Do you feel different while you're wearing the mask?
- Does wearing a mask change who you are inside?

Paper Bag Wigs

Help your child develop their imagination.

You'll Need

- Medium-sized paper bags
- Scissors
- Glue
- Yarn
- Markers
- Ribbons and bows
- Old sunglasses (optional)

Directions

1. Cut the front of the bag to frame your child's face. Make "hair" by cutting the paper into thin strips all around. To make curly hair, show your child how to curl the strips around a pencil.

2. Your child may want to add a hair bow or add yarn to make different colored hair.

Things to Talk About

- How is this "wig" different from your hair?
- Do you like changing the way your hair looks?

If you have sunglasses, your child might like to pretend they are a spy.

Rhythm Rattles

Help your child express their feelings through music.

You'll Need

- Cardboard tubes from wrapping paper, aluminum foil or paper towels
- Wax paper
- Rubber bands
- Beads or pebbles
- Markers
- Glue (optional)
- Tissue paper (optional)
- Yarn (optional)

This could be a good Recycling Project (page 57).

Directions

1. Show your child how to make a rattle by covering one end of the tube with wax paper and securing it with a rubber band. Have your child pour a handful of beads or pebbles in the tube, then help them cover the other end with wax paper and a rubber band.

2. Let your child play with the rattle and make their own musical rhythm. Let your child decorate their rattle with the paper, yarn and glue, if they'd like.

Things to Talk About

- Do you know what a rattle is?
- Do you like dancing to music?

Shaving Cream Finger Painting

Help your child develop creative play.

When done, have your child help you clean up with warm water and a sponge.

You'll Need

- Shaving cream
- Trays or washable surface
- Apron or old shirt

Directions

1. Give your child a tray to work on or set them up at an easily washable surface. Give then an apron or old shirt to put on to protect their clothes.

2. Give your child a small amount of shaving cream and let them spread it around on their work surface.

Things to Talk About

- Can you make different designs with the sides of your hands? What about your fingertips or knuckles?

Paper Chain Decorations

Help your child develop muscle control and fine motor coordination.

You'll Need

- An assortment of colored construction paper
- Safety scissors
- Glue or tape

Directions

1. Help your child cut five or six narrow strips from the construction paper.

2. Show your child how to make a loop and glue or tape it together. Make a chain by inserting another strip into this loop then gluing its ends together. Add as many loops as you'd like.

Things to Talk About

- Was this chain easy to put together?
- Would you like to practice making more strips?

Your child may want to hang the chain up once it's finished.

Bird Puppets

Help your child use their imagination.

You'll Need

- Drinking straws
- Magazine pictures or printouts of different kinds of birds
- Construction paper
- Markers
- Glue
- Tape

Directions

1. Show your child how to make a bird stick puppet by cutting out the pictures, gluing them on construction paper and taping them to the straws.

2. Let your child pretend to make the birds fly, look for worms, etc.

Things to Talk About

- How are the birds the same?
- How are they different?

Your child might also like to make a stick puppet of a bird they drew.

Museum of Love

Help your child express their feelings through artwork.

You'll Need

- Paper
- Markers or crayons
- Paint and brushes (optional)

Directions

1. Help your child make a list of the people and things they love: family members, friends, pets, a special toy, etc.

2. Have your child choose a few of these subjects to draw or paint. Once they are done, hang their pictures up on the wall to make a small "exhibit."

Things to Talk About

- Have you been to a museum?
- Do you think art is a good way to show your feelings?

You can also mount the pictures on construction paper to make "frames."

Soap Sculptures

Help your child develop creative play.

You'll Need

- Bar of soap
- Vegetable peeler
- Box of tissues
- Large bowl
- Water

Directions

1. Have your child rip up about 15 tissues into small pieces and put them in the bowl. Then, by yourself or with your child's help, shave about half of the soap into the tissues with the vegetable peeler.

2. Add 1/3 cup of water to the bowl and let your child stir it. Add more water, 1 tablespoon at a time, until the mixture is of molding consistency—it will feel like mud when it's ready.

3. Let your child sculpt whatever they'd like out of the mixture. It will hold its shape, but won't harden. If it dries out, add a few drops of water to make it pliable again.

Things to Talk About

- Do you like the feel of the "clay?"
- What kinds of things can you make with it?

Remind your child this is still soap and not to touch their eyes while working with it.

63

Chalk Skywriting

Help your child learn about new concepts.

You'll Need

- Blue, gray or dark construction paper
- White chalk

Directions

1. Ask your child to pretend they are the pilot of a skywriting airplane. What would they write in the sky?

2. Let your child use the chalk to make their "skywriting."

Things to Talk About

- Have you ever seen skywriting before? What did it look like?

You may want to show your child a video of a pilot writing in the sky.

Three-Cornered Collage

Help your child learn about the world around them.

You'll Need

- Construction paper
- Glue
- Paper, cut into triangle shapes
- Scrap materials (more paper, ribbons, cotton balls, yarn, etc.)

Directions

1. Ask your child if they know what a triangle is. Can they point out anything in the room shaped like a triangle?

2. Give your child a few triangle shapes and let them glue them to their construction paper. (They can cut this into a triangle too!) Let them add other items to their collage as they please.

Things to Talk About

- How many sides and corners do triangles have?
- What are other shapes called?

You could also do this activity with circles, squares, rectangles or diamonds.

When you're done, have your child help you clean up, pick up, put away!

Games

Practice coordination, sharing and more while playing along!

Tightrope Walking

Help your child develop coordination and the ability to keep on trying.

If your child finds this easy, they can try walking backward.

You'll Need

- Two 6-foot pieces of string or masking tape
- Tape to fasten string

Directions

1. Make a "tightrope" by taping a long piece of string or masking tape to the floor. Show your child how to walk on it in a straight line by putting one foot in front of the other. If your child has trouble walking on the line, you can place a second one down about 4 inches away from the first one and they can practice walking between the two lines.

Things to Talk About

- Do you know what balance is?
- Is it better to go fast or slow when you're trying to walk on the tightrope?

It's Too Noisy

Help your child develop self-control.

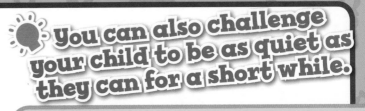
You can also challenge your child to be as quiet as they can for a short while.

You'll Need

- Nothing

Directions

1. Ask your child if they can think of a time when something was too noisy. Some ideas: a car alarm, fireworks, a loud parade.

2. Agree on a signal that means "quiet," like flicking the lights on and off. Then let your child make a lot of noise—clapping, singing, stomping feet. But they need to stop when you give the signal!

Things to Talk About

- Can you think of a time when an adult said you were being too noisy?

- Why do we need to be quiet sometimes?

Outline Match

Help your child learn to look carefully and recognize likeness and difference.

You'll Need

- Large sheet of paper

- Markers

- Assorted objects (block, key, toy car, coin, coloring book)

- Pots and pans with lids, assorted plastic containers with lids (optional)

Directions

1. Have your child help you trace the various objects on the paper. Then mix up the objects and ask your child to match each to its outline.

Things to Talk About

- How can you tell where something fits?

- Can you name all the objects just by their outlines?

Younger children might enjoy matching pots, pans and plastic containers with their lids.

Questions

Help your child feel comfortable asking about what they need to know.

You'll Need

- Nothing

Directions

1. Play a simple version of Twenty Questions. Choose an object in the room, and let your child ask questions to guess which object you're thinking of. You can suggest questions to them, such as what the color is, whether it's big or little, etc.

Things to Talk About

- Explain to your child that asking questions is a good way to find out what you need to know.

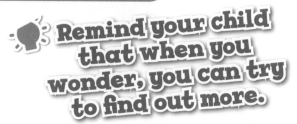

Remind your child that when you wonder, you can try to find out more.

Familiar Sounds

Help your child learn to listen carefully.

You'll Need

- Keys
- Paper
- Ball
- Measuring spoons
- Water
- Pitcher
- Cup

Directions

1. Have your child turn around while you make different noises and see if they can identify them. You can knock on a door, stomp your feet, rattle keys, clap your hands, pour water, bounce a ball, jingle measuring spoons, etc.

Things to Talk About

- Do some things sound more similar than others?
- Why is listening important?

You could also look up different sound effects and animal noises online.

Fishing

Help your child develop the ability to keep on trying.

You'll Need

- Magnet
- String
- Pencil or ruler
- Bucket
- Fish shapes cut from heavy paper
- Paper clips
- Scissors

Directions

1. Place the paper clips on the fish and put them in the bucket. Tie a magnet to a ruler to make a "fishing rod."

2. Let your child try to pick up the fish with the magnet.

Things to Talk About

- Do you know what a magnet is?
- Is it easier to do this after you've had some practice?

Write down directions on each fish that must be done as it's caught, like "hop on one foot" or "jump three times."

Hide It, Find It
Help your child develop healthy curiosity.

You'll Need

- Small block or toy
- Box
- Scarf
- Paper bag
- Pillow

Directions

1. Show your child the toy and the hiding places you might put it: in the box, under the scarf, in the bag or under the pillow.

2. Have your child turn around or cover their eyes while you hide the toy, then let them look for it. Older children may like to ask some questions before they look for the toy.

Things to Talk About

- Is the toy under something?
- Is it in something?
- Is the hiding place made of paper or cloth?

If you are doing this activity with more than one child, they might like to take turns hiding the toy.

Rolling

Help your child develop coordination and muscle control.

You'll Need

- Several blankets

Directions

1. Make a mat for your child by spreading several blankets on the floor.

2. Show your child how to roll over the length of the blankets.

3. Let your child roll over the blankets, stopping them when they reach the end.

Things to Talk About

- Have you ever seen someone doing gymnastics?

- Do you think they could do cartwheels and flips right away?

 **This activity could also be done on a grassy lawn.**

Quiet Place

Help your child develop self-control and practice waiting.

You'll Need

- Kitchen timer or phone stopwatch

Directions

1. Set the timer for 15 seconds and ask your child to sit on the floor as quietly as possible until the timer rings. When the timer goes off, then they can make noise.

2. Set the timer again and repeat the activity for 20 seconds, then 30 seconds if you think they can wait that long.

 **This can be a good game to play in the car (as long as you're not driving).**

Things to Talk About

- Was it hard to sit very still?

- Do you feel proud for staying quiet?

- What did you think about while you were waiting?

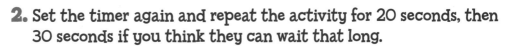

In the Bag

Help your child learn to look carefully and develop their memory.

You'll Need

- 3 identical paper bags (like lunch bags)
- Small common objects (paper clip, rubber bands, blocks, etc.)

Directions

1. While your child watches, place one object in each of the bags.

2. While your child is still watching, switch the bags around.

3. Ask your child to guess where one of the objects is now.

If your child is a little older, make this game harder by moving more quickly when you switch the bags around.

Things to Talk About

- Can you remember where the object was when the game started?
- Which objects are in the other bags?

Use Your Breath

Help your child learn more about their body and develop coordination.

You'll Need

- Styrofoam balls, ping-pong balls or clean crumpled tissues
- Straws
- Masking tape

Directions

1. Give your child a straw and show them how to blow through it. Show them how they can feel the air if they put a hand at the other end of the straw.

2. Give them balls and let them see what happens when they blow air at them.

3. Make a path across any smooth surface using two strips of masking tape. Let your child practice moving the ball down the path.

Your child might also like trying to blow a ball across a table without letting it fall on the floor.

Things to Talk About

- Does this become easier to do the more you practice?
- Do you think your breath could move something heavier, like a baseball?

Snow Statues

Help your child develop muscle control and their imagination.

You'll Need

- Nothing

Things to Talk About

- What other sports could you pretend to play?
- What do you think about while you are "frozen?"

Directions

1. Let your child pretend to be doing an activity like playing tennis, swimming or playing basketball.

2. Tell your child that when you say "freeze," they must stop what they are doing and stand as still as a statue. When you say "unfreeze," they can continue pretending.

Small children might like to just be dancing or singing a song before they "freeze."

75

Magic Exercises

Help your child understand the difference between real and pretend.

You'll Need

- Nothing

Your child might like a magic book to see how some common "magic" tricks work.

Directions

1. Have your child think of a chore that they wish could be done by magic—making their bed, picking up their toys, putting away clothes, etc.

2. Come up with a "magic" exercise to do this chore. It might be standing on their toes, waving a pretend wand, saying a magic word, wishing hard, etc.

3. Try the magic exercises to complete the chore.

Things to Talk About

- Did the magic exercise work? Why not?

- How else can we make sure chores get done?

Balancing Blocks

Help your child develop coordination and muscle control.

You'll Need

- Building blocks

Directions

1. Let your child see how high they can stack the blocks. Then have them try to balance blocks in their hand. Can they balance more than one at a time?

2. Your child might also like to practice balancing themself. Can they stand on their tiptoes and count to 10? Hop up and down on one foot and then the other?

Things to Talk About

- Does standing on your tiptoes get easier the more you do it?

- Do you like practicing new things?

You might like to sing "Keep Trying" (lyrics on page 279).

Guess What's Inside

Help your child recognize likeness and difference.

You'll Need

- Pillowcase
- Common household objects, like a comb, brush, pencil, spoon, crayon, etc.

Directions

1. Put everything inside the pillowcase.

2. Let your child reach inside and feel an object. Can they guess what it is based on touch? Once they have a guess, they can pull it out and see if they were right.

You might want to show your child the objects before you put them in the pillowcase if they are very young.

Things to Talk About

- Is the object narrow? Soft? Hard?

- What do you think it's made of?

Puzzles

Help your child develop their memory and learn to keep trying.

You'll Need

- Pictures of cars, toys or other objects
- Safety scissors
- Construction paper
- Glue

Directions

1. Help your child choose a picture and glue it to a piece of construction paper.

2. After the glue has dried, let your child cut the picture into five or six pieces.

3. Mix up the pieces and let your child try to put the picture back together again.

It's best to choose pictures of inanimate objects—some children might feel anxious cutting up pictures of people or animals.

Things to Talk About

- Do you remember what the picture looked like before you cut it up?

- What was it a picture of?

Animal Sounds

Help your child learn more about their world and practice listening carefully.

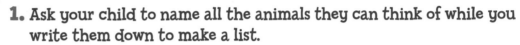

You might want to show your child a video of these animals making noises.

You'll Need

- Paper
- Pencil, pen or marker

Directions

1. Ask your child to name all the animals they can think of while you write them down to make a list.

2. Once you are done making a list, read off the name of each animal and see if your child knows what sound it makes.

Things to Talk About

- Are there different ways to sound like the same animal?
- Are there any animals that don't make sounds?
- How do you think they communicate?

What's Missing?

Help your child learn to look carefully.

You'll Need

- 5 or 6 small objects (toy car, brush, block, ball, comb, crayon, spoon, etc.)

Directions

1. Show your child the items you have chosen. Make sure your child can name all of them.

2. Spread the items out on a table or the floor and let your child look at them carefully for a few minutes.

3. Ask your child to close their eyes while you take one of the objects away. Can they tell what's missing?

Things to Talk About

- What color was the missing object?
- Do you remember where it was on the table?

Have your child help put each object away at the end of the activity.

79

Stop Sign

Help your child learn about limits and develop self-control.

 You can also challenge your child to be quiet for a short while.

You'll Need

- Paper
- Markers
- Yardstick or old broom handle
- Tape

Things to Talk About

- Why is it important to follow directions?
- What do stop signs on the street mean?

Directions

1. Make a large "stop" sign out of paper and then tape it to the yardstick; then make a "go" sign and tape it on the other side.

2. Tell your child that when the "go" side is facing them, they must move, and when the "stop" side is facing them, they must stop. You can play this game while your child is dancing, hopping or playing with cars and trucks.

Make Your Own Games

Help your child develop creative play and coordination.

You'll Need

• Game spinner from an old game, or a set of dice
• Wastebasket
• Balls or beanbags

Directions

1. Tell your child that you're going to make up your own game with these objects. You can suggest a few things first—maybe they would like to roll the dice to see how many times they should hop, clap hands or throw a ball. Or they can try to toss beanbags into a wastebasket.

2. Have your child come up with a game they can play by themself or with other children.

Things to Talk About

• Do you like coming up with new things to do?

• Are there any other objects you can use to make up a new game?

Can You Find the Toy?

Help your child develop the ability to keep trying.

You'll Need

• Box of sand
• Small toys (car, doll, spoon, block, etc.)

Directions

1. Show all the toys to your child, then hide one in the sand.

2. Let your child try to find the toy by feeling. Once they find it, you can try hiding two toys at once.

Things to Talk About

• Can you tell which toy it is just by feeling?

• What do you do when you can't find one of your toys in your room?

If you don't have sand, you can put the toys under a blanket to hide them.

Trying on Hats
Help your child try out different roles.

You'll Need

- An assortment of hats
- Pictures of people in different kinds of hats

Directions

1. Let your child try on the different kinds of hats or look at the pictures of people in different hats. As you look at each one, have your child name the kind of person who might wear a hat like that. Some ideas are a cap for a baseball player, a red hat for a firefighter or a fancy hat for going to a party.

Things to Talk About

- Why do you think we have different kinds of hats?
- Do chefs have special hats?
- What about police officers?

Your child might like to make up a story about where they are going in their hat.

Mirror, Mirror on the Wall

Help your child learn to pay attention.

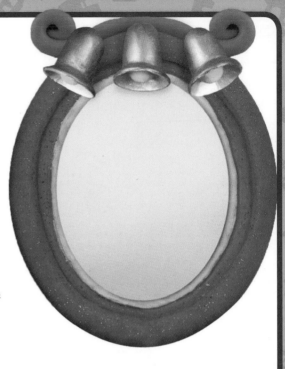

You'll Need

• Mirror

Your child might like to look for other places to see their reflection, like a shiny door, window or rain puddle.

Directions

1. Have your child look at themself, preferably in a full-length mirror. Ask them to follow simple directions while looking in the mirror. Can they point to their nose? Cover their eyes? Touch their feet? Raise their arms?

Things to Talk About

• Do you know what a reflection is?

• Where else can you see your reflection?

Find the Timer

Help your child learn to listen carefully.

You'll Need

• Kitchen timer or loud-ticking alarm clock

Directions

1. Set the timer to go off in 5 minutes, then hide it somewhere in the room. Ask your child to try to find it before the alarm goes off.

Things to Talk About

• Can you remember not being able to find something?

• Were you able to find it again?

• If not, what do you think happened to it?

If you are playing this game with more than one child, they might like to take turns hiding the timer.

Peekaboo

Help your child use play to work on feelings.

You'll Need

- Scarf or soft blanket

Directions

1. Cover a doll with a blanket. Wait a few moments, then pull it off.

2. Now cover your own head. You might want to say something like "Where am I?" while you are hidden, then take off the blanket.

3. Ask your child if they would like to cover their head with the blanket.

Things to Talk About

- Do you know any other ways to play peekaboo?

- Do you really disappear when you're under the blanket?

Show your child a video of a magician disappearing. Remind them that it's a trick—people and objects don't really disappear.

Painting with Water

Help your child develop their imagination.

You'll Need

- Water
- Buckets
- Brushes
- Something to paint (the porch, railings, lawn furniture, etc.)

Directions

1. If your child has expressed interest in helping you do an adult task—like painting walls or furniture—they might like to "pretend" paint.

2. Give your child a bucket of water and an old paint brush to use on things like the porch, steps, railings or other water-safe surfaces.

Things to Talk About

- What "color" are you painting with?
- Do you want to pretend to be a house painter?

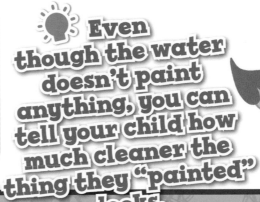 

Even though the water doesn't paint anything, you can tell your child how much cleaner the thing they "painted" looks.

Makeup

Help your child understand the difference between real and pretend.

You'll Need

- Old makeup or costume makeup
- Cold cream or petroleum jelly
- Wig or hat
- Washcloths
- Soap and water

Directions

1. Let your child use the makeup to change their appearance. They might like to make a pretty face, clown or monster.

2. Let your child try on a wig or hat too.

3. When your child is done, help them remove the makeup with cold cream or petroleum jelly.

Things to Talk About

- Did the makeup change who you are underneath?
- Was it fun to look different?

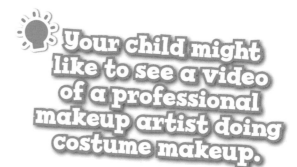

Your child might like to see a video of a professional makeup artist doing costume makeup.

Bubble Play

Help your child develop creative play and express feelings through movement.

You'll Need

- Water
- Dishwashing liquid
- String (foot-long pieces)
- Plastic bowl
- Soft music (optional)

Directions

1. Add a cup of mild dishwashing liquid and a quart of warm water to a large plastic bowl. Tie a piece of foot-long string into a loop and let your child dip it into the soapy water.

2. Show your child how to blow through the loop to make a bubble. When the bubble play is over, your child might like to make up a "bubble dance."

Things to Talk About

- Can your child show you how a bubble floats in the air?
- Can they pretend to be a bubble that pops?
- What about a bubble just floating to music?

 This is a good outdoor activity.

Let Me Find You

Help your child work on feelings about separation.

You might want to end this activity by reading a book together or holding hands so you are "connected" again.

You'll Need

- A safe hiding area (part of the house or a fenced-in yard)

Directions

1. Ask your child to find a hiding space in your house or yard while you turn around and count to 20.

2. Try to find your child, but take your time. Children enjoy the game more when you pretend not to be able to find them at first.

Things to Talk About

- Did you think I was going to be able to find you?

- Do you want to trade places so you look for me?

If I Had a Pet

Help your child develop their imagination and learn to use their words.

You'll Need

- Paper
- Crayons or markers

Directions

1. Ask your child to make up a pet they would like to have, but not to tell you what it is yet.

2. Ask your child questions to guess what the pet is.

3. Ask your child if they would like to draw a picture of their pretend pet. Do they have a name for it?

Remind your child that a pretend pet can be any animal, like an elephant or dinosaur.

Things to Talk About

- Does it have fur? If yes, is it long or short?

- How many legs does it have?

- How would you take care of it?

Trying on Shoes

Help your child develop creative play and learn more about money.

You'll Need

- 4 or 5 pairs of shoes
- Shoeboxes
- Chair
- Ruler
- Paper or plastic bags
- Play money

Directions

1. Tell your child you're going to go pretend-shopping for a new pair of shoes.

2. Act out a scene where you measure your child's feet, let them pick out a pair of shoes and try them on. Let your child use the play money to "purchase" the shoes, which you can then box up and put in a bag for them.

> If you have more than one child, they might like to take turns being the customer and salesperson.

Things to Talk About

- Do you remember when you really bought these shoes?
- What did you have to give the store so you could take them home?

Musical Jars

Help your child learn to listen carefully and recognize likeness and difference.

You'll need

- 5 or 6 glass jars
- Pitcher of water
- Spoon or pencil

Directions

1. See if your child can handle a pitcher well enough to fill the glass jars, putting a different amount of water in each one.

2. Show your child what happens when they tap the glass with a fork or pencil. Let them tap the jars to make different sounds.

Things to Talk About

- How are the sounds different?
- Which jar has the highest sound? The lowest?

If you have dry-erase markers, you can make lines showing how high the water comes up in each jar.

What's Under the Towel?

Help your child learn to look carefully and feel comfortable asking questions.

You'll Need

- 5–10 medium-sized objects (cereal box, saucepan, baby doll, plastic pitcher, empty juice carton, etc.)
- Bath towel

Directions

1. Show your child each of the items you've selected for this game and make sure they know the name for each item. Now hide the items and explain that when they close their eyes, you are going to choose one item to put under the towel.

2. Have your child guess what is under the towel. See if they can guess just by looking at the shape. If they can't, have them ask questions to help them figure out what the item is.

Things to Talk About

- Is the object soft?
- Do you use it to play with?
- What room does it belong in?

Younger children might like to feel under the towel when guessing the object.

Stop-and-Go Game

Help your child develop muscle control and self-control.

This is a good game for a group.

You'll Need

- Music

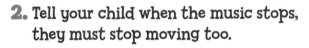

Directions

1. Play some music for your child to move and dance to.

2. Tell your child when the music stops, they must stop moving too.

3. After about 30 seconds, stop the music. Keep it stopped for 5 to 10 seconds, then begin playing it again. Keep playing for as long as you'd like.

Things to Talk About

- Can you hold the exact position you were in when the music stopped?

- What do you think about when you're not dancing?

Toss Game

Help your child practice taking turns and developing coordination.

You'll Need

- 2–3 paper plates
- A few bottle caps

Older children can stand farther back to make this activity more difficult.

Directions

1. Place the plates close to one another on the floor. Stand a few feet away and take turns tossing the bottle caps one at a time, aiming for the plates.

2. After a couple of practice rounds, your child might like counting how many caps landed on the plates and how many landed on the floor each turn.

Things to Talk About

- Why is it good to take turns?
- What can you do while you're waiting?

Cover Your Eyes

Help your child develop the ability to keep trying.

Things to Talk About

- Which tasks were the easiest to do? The hardest?

You'll Need

- Pencil
- Paper
- Box or grocery bag
- Blindfold

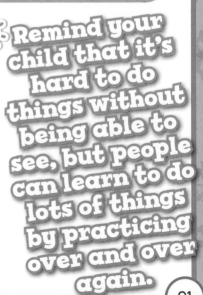

Directions

1. Have your child try to complete a few different everyday tasks while wearing a blindfold. They could try to button a sweater, put on a hat, sweep the floor, etc.

2. Have your child try to make a drawing while their eyes are covered. You may wish to place a piece of paper inside a shallow box for this task.

Remind your child that it's hard to do things without being able to see, but people can learn to do lots of things by practicing over and over again.

Spin the Number

Help your child practice working together and taking turns.

You'll Need

- Cardboard or heavy paper
- Markers
- Scissors
- Brass paper fastener

Directions

1. Cut a 5- or 6-inch circle from cardboard or heavy paper and divide it into six sections with a marker. Write a numeral (1-6) in each section. Make a 3-inch arrow from the leftover paper and attach it to the circle using a brass paper fastener. Loosen the arrow if necessary so it spins easily.

2. Use this homemade spinner to make up a game with your child. You might want to spin it and jump that many times; spin a number and find that many things that are round (or square or blue); or bounce a ball or clap your hands the number of times the spinner shows.

Things to Talk About

- What else can we do with the spinner?

- How many people can use the spinner at one time?

Older children might like to make a simple board game to use with the spinner.

Where's the Peanut?

Help your child develop their memory skills and work on feelings about separation.

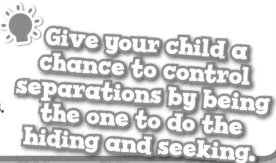

You'll Need

- 3 paper cups
- Bag of peanuts (in the shell)

Things to Talk About

- Remind your child that sometimes you have to go out, but grownups come back.

Directions

1. You may want to start this activity by talking to your child about how they feel when you are at work or running errands and they can't come with you.

2. Show your child the bag of peanuts and point out their different shapes and sizes. Ask your child to close their eyes while you hide a peanut under one of the cups, then let your child guess which cup the peanut is under.

3. Once they have guessed correctly, let them hide the peanut while you or another child guesses.

Give your child a chance to control separations by being the one to do the hiding and seeking.

Bagball

Help your child develop coordination and learn about conservation.

You'll Need

- Empty paper grocery bag
- Soft stuffed ball

Things to Talk About

- What are some other uses for an empty paper bag?

Directions

1. Fold down the top edge of a grocery bag about 1 inch all around to help the bag stand up more easily by itself. Let your child play by tossing the soft ball into the bag, or "bowling" the ball in if the bag falls over. If you don't have a soft ball, you can use a balled up pair of socks.

This is also a good opportunity to practice taking turns.

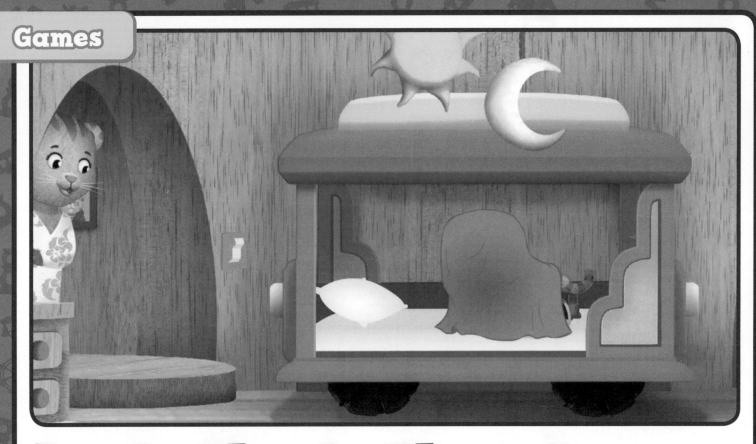

Look, Think, Then Guess

Help your child work on feelings about separation and learn more about the world.

You'll Need

- Several familiar toys
- Scarf or small lightweight blanket

Directions

1. Let your child see and feel the toys you have selected for this game.

2. Ask them to close their eyes, then hide one of the toys under the scarf. See if your child can guess which toy has been hidden.

3. If your child can't guess right away, let them feel through the cover and then under it.

Things to Talk About

- Do you remember the three toys I showed you?

- How can you tell which toy is under the blanket?

This is a good game to play with multiple children so they can take turns hiding the toys and guessing.

Where's the Bird?

Help your child use play to work on feelings and develop the ability to keep trying.

You'll Need

- Toy bird or small picture of a bird

Directions

1. Hide the bird while having your child cover their eyes. Once it's hidden, have your child look for the bird while you give them hints about where to look.

2. Once your child has found the bird, let them take a turn at hiding it.

Things to Talk About
- Could you see the bird right away?
- How did you feel when you found it?

You can tell your child they are getting "warmer" or "colder" while they are looking.

Fast and Slow, Then Stop

Help your child develop self-control and coordination.

You'll Need
- Speaker
- Music

Things to Talk About
- Is it harder to stop when you're doing something quickly?

Directions

1. Choose a few songs that are fast and a few songs that are slow in tempo. Let your child listen to both kinds of music, encouraging them to move to the beat of each one.

2. Play a game where your child moves when the music plays, but they must stop when the music stops. Start with the slow music, then play the fast music.

Ending the game with slow music may help your child calm down.

95

Your child might enjoy seeing a video of cement being used in construction.

Pretend Cement

Help your child develop their imagination.

You'll Need

- Sand and water, or
- Salt, flour and water
- Containers

Things to Talk About

- What does the "cement" feel like?
- What happens when it dries?

Directions

1. If the weather is nice, give your child a container with sand and water inside and let them mix it to make "cement." They can pour it in the yard or pretend to fill cracks in a driveway or porch.

2. If playing indoors, mix 1 cup salt with 2 cups flour and add ½ cup cold water. Mix with your hands for homemade modeling clay. Roll it out and let your child make a print with their hands, fingers or feet. After several hours, the clay will harden like real cement.

Blowing Bubbles

Help your child develop creative play.

You'll Need

- Straws
- Bowls
- Dish soap
- Bubble wands (optional)

Directions

1. Add soap to a half-full bowl of water and show your child how to make bubbles by blowing into a straw in the bowl. Make sure they practice blowing out of a straw before letting them do so in the bowl.

2. If you can, go outside afterward and use a bubble wand to make bubbles that float in the air.

Things to Talk About

- What is inside the bubbles?
- What happens when you touch them?

If you don't have a bubble wand, use a wire hanger to make very large bubbles!

Boxes Inside Boxes

Help your child learn more about their world.

You'll Need

- 5–6 boxes of graduated sizes so each box fits into the box of the next size larger (ring box, popcorn box, shirt box, etc.)
- Small toy that will fit into the smallest box

Directions

1. Without your child knowing, place the toy inside the smallest box, then place each box inside the other.

2. Give the boxes to your child to open. If doing this with more than one child, have them take turns opening the boxes.

3. After the smallest box is opened, come up with ideas of what to do with the boxes.

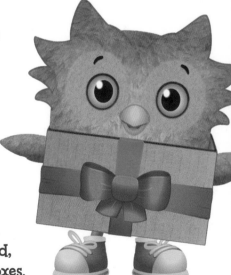

Things to Talk About

- Do you want to put the boxes back together?
- Do you want to build something with the boxes?

Your child might surprise you with their own idea of what to do with the boxes.

Keys

Help your child learn more about their world and understand likeness and difference.

You'll Need

- Keys
- Locks
- Pencils
- Paper

Directions

1. Show your child a few different keys. Point out how the edges are different on different keys. Explain that most keys only fit one lock. Let them see how a key can open a door, a car trunk or a locked box, if you have one.

2. Trace all the different keys on a piece of paper and have your child try to match each key to its tracing.

You might like to give your child a set of play keys or keys made from cardboard for pretending.

Things to Talk About

- Do you know what a key is for?
- How are all the keys alike?
- How are they different?

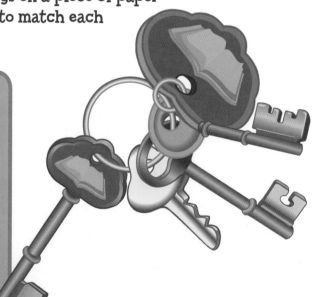

Caterpillars and Butterflies

Help your child learn more about growing.

You'll Need

- Scarves and bath towels in assorted colors

Directions

1. Have your child pretend to be a caterpillar. Let them show you how they crawl around.

2. Have your child lay very still and wrap a scarf or towel around them to make a cocoon. Wait a moment, then encourage them to come out and emerge as a butterfly.

3. Your child might like to use a scarf as wings as they "fly."

Things to Talk About

- Do you know what a caterpillar is?

- Do you know what it becomes? What else changes as it grows?

You might like to show your child a video or book about metamorphosis after playing this game.

Stilts

Help your child develop coordination and the ability to keep on trying.

You'll Need

- 16-oz plastic yogurt tubs, or similar plastic tubs (2 for each child)

- Long pieces of heavy string

- Sharp knife or scissors

Directions

1. Turn the tubs upside down and use a sharp knife or scissors to make holes on two sides of each container. See if your child can thread a piece of string through the holes in each tub.

2. With the tubs upside down on the floor, tie the ends of the string together to make a loop that is about waist-high for your child. Can your child stand on the tubs and, keeping the string tight, walk around as if on stilts?

Things to Talk About

- Is it easy to walk like this?

- Is there anything you can see better while you are taller?

Walk, Crawl and Hop

Help your child learn about limits and develop the ability to keep on trying.

You'll Need

- Masking tape or chalk
- Large cardboard box
- 2–3 shoeboxes
- 2 egg cartons

Directions

1. Set up an obstacle course in your yard or a room with lots of space. Use masking tape to make a pretend tightrope, place the shoeboxes far enough apart for your child to step over, open the ends of the large box to make a tunnel and place the egg cartons so they can be hopped over.

2. Tell your child they need to walk along the "tightrope," step over the boxes, crawl through the tunnel and then hop over the egg cartons. Can they follow the rules?

Later on, switch things around or make up new rules to make a new course to try.

Things to Talk About

- Do you get better each time you try the obstacle course?
- Is it difficult to remember all the rules?

Trolley Tracks

Help your child develop their imagination and coordination.

Your child might like to add roads for cars and trucks.

You'll Need

- Several paper grocery bags or an old sheet
- Blocks or boxes
- Cardboard circles to use as wheels
- Tape
- Markers

Directions

1. Tape several large paper grocery bags together or spread an old sheet on the floor.

2. With a marker, draw a set of trolley tracks on the paper or sheet. If your child is older, they might like to help with the drawing.

3. Small boxes or blocks can be used as pretend trolleys by taping cardboard wheels on the sides.

Things to Talk About

- Where is your trolley going?
- Is there anything else you want to add to the play mat?

Homemade Instruments

Help your child express their feelings through music.

This is a good activity for a group of children.

You'll Need

- Paper towel tubes
- Pots and pans
- Wooden spoons
- Metal spoons
- String
- Rubber bands
- Yogurt tubs
- Paper plates
- Beads

Directions

1. Your child might like to use the materials to make Cardboard Trumpets (page 17), Paper Plate Shakers (page 41), Rhythm Rattles (page 60) or another instrument of their own making.

2. Encourage your child to try out their instrument. Using another homemade instrument, play with them as a small band or orchestra.

Things to Talk About

- What kind of music does each instrument make?
- What happens when different people play different instruments at the same time?

A Medical Play Kit

Help your child use play to work on feelings and try out different roles.

You'll Need

- Smock or old white shirt
- Tongue depressors
- Bandages (strips of cloth)

Directions

1. Have your child help you collect materials to make a medical kit: a yardstick or tape measure to see how much they've grown, an old pen (without the ink cartridge) for giving pretend injections, a bubble wand for a pretend stethoscope.

2. Let your child put on the smock and pretend to give you or another child a checkup.

Your child might also like the Playing Doctor Daniel game on pbskids.org.

Things to Talk About

- Can you remember a time when you went to the doctor?
- What was the examination like?

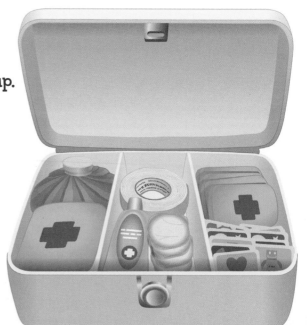

102

Marble Roll

Help your child develop creative play and coordination.

You'll Need

- Paper towel tubes
- Small milk cartons or juice boxes
- Marbles or ping-pong balls

Directions

1. Set out the materials and show your child how to roll the marble through the paper towel tube.

2. Help your child make an obstacle course for the ball. Your child might like watching how it bounces off all the different objects.

Things to Talk About

- Are there any other things we could add to our obstacle course?
- What happens if you roll the ball more quickly?

If your child is very young, you might prefer to use ping-pong balls so you don't have to worry about them swallowing a marble.

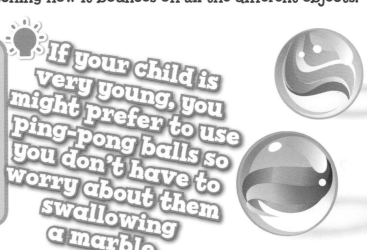

What's Missing?

Help your child learn to look carefully and develop their memory.

You'll Need

- Collection of household items or small toys (e.g. key, spoon, toy car, ribbon, block, pencil, etc.)

Directions

1. Arrange five to 10 items on a tray and have your child name them all. While you or another child closes their eyes, have your child remove one of the items from the tray.

2. Whoever closed their eyes must guess what was removed from the tray. Take turns so everyone gets a chance at removing an item.

Things to Talk About

- How do you feel when something changes?
- Does it take some time to get used to new things?

Nesting Toys

Help your child develop coordination.

You'll Need

- Assortment of objects that fit inside one another (coin purse, cosmetic bag, purse, tote bag, shopping bag)
- Toy that fits inside the smallest bag or purse
- Paper envelopes of different sizes
- Paper
- Scissors
- Markers
- Cardboard
- Glue

Directions

1. Make a set of nesting toys by placing each bag inside the next-largest bag. Let your child open everything to reach the toy in the smallest bag.

2. Have your child make their own nesting game by drawing a small picture and placing it in the smallest envelope, which then can be placed in a larger one and so on.

Things to Talk About

- Can a large bag fit inside a small one?
- Can you put everything back the way it was before you opened all the bags?

Your child might like to see a video or book about traditional Russian nesting dolls.

Pocket Comb Harmonica

Help your child develop creative play and express feelings through music.

You'll Need

- Clean pocket comb
- Wax paper

Directions

1. Help your child fold a small piece of wax paper over the comb (let the open side show the comb's teeth). Show them how to hum through the teeth of the comb to make a sound like a kazoo.

2. Encourage your child to play music that expresses different feelings.

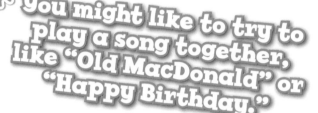

You might like to try to play a song together, like "Old MacDonald" or "Happy Birthday."

Things to Talk About

- Can you play happy music? Sad music? Angry music?

Walking the Line

If this is too difficult, try Tightrope Walking (page 68).

Help your child develop the ability to keep trying.

You'll Need

- Masking tape or chalk

Directions

1. Make a "balance beam" by putting a long length of masking tape on the floor. If you are outside, you may wish to draw a long chalk line.

2. Show your child how to walk straight down the line by putting one foot in front of the other and walking heel to toe.

3. Let your child practice this. If it gets too easy, they might like to walk backward or sideways.

Things to Talk About

- What is balance?
- Can you do this while holding your arms straight out at your sides?
- Does it get easier the more you do it?

Tunnels and Bridges

Help your child develop creative play.

You'll Need

- Empty cardboard tubes
- Oatmeal boxes with both ends removed
- Toy cars
- Toy people or animals
- Blocks or small cardboard boxes

Directions

1. Set out the materials and let your child play with them. If they don't do this on their own, show your child how to use one of the tubes as a tunnel for a toy car and how a box can make a bridge over the tunnel.

2. Young children might enjoy pulling cars and other toys through the tunnels by pulling on a piece of string you've attached to them.

Things to Talk About

- What else can you use to make tunnels?

- What else could you use the boxes for?

If you have a sandbox, cover the tubes with sand to make tunnels for the cars.

Up and Down Pulleys

Help your child develop their imagination.

You'll Need

- Small basket with handle
- Heavy string
- Wooden dowel
- Toy animals or people

Things to Talk About

- What do you think people use pulleys for?
- Can you think of other times you've seen one?

Directions

1. To make a pulley, tie the string to the handle of a small basket and place the toys in the basket. Then use two chairs to support the ends of the dowel (a broomstick works too) and loop the string over the dowel.

2. Let your child pull the string and see how the basket is lifted up.

💡 You may be able to set this up as an elevator outside a dollhouse or other toy building.

Toy Car Wash

Help your child learn more about their world.

You'll Need

- Clean milk cartons or cardboard tubes
- Toy cars that fit inside cartons or tubes

💡 This could be a good activity to do alongside Trolley Tracks (page 101).

Directions

1. If you are using a carton, open or cut off both ends so the toy car can be "driven" through. Let your child set up a car wash for pretend play. They might like to make washing noises or tape two cartons together and add ribbon or yarn in between for the car to drive through.

Things to Talk About

- Have you ever been in a car wash?
- How else do people wash their cars?

An Ambulance for the Dolls

Help your child use play to work on feelings.

You'll Need

- Pillowcase or towel
- Toy medical kit
- Strips of cloth for bandages
- Medical dress-up clothes
- Dolls or stuffed animals

Directions

1. Show your child how to set up a pretend ambulance with the dolls as patients and your child as the paramedic. A pillowcase or towel can be the stretcher.

2. Let your child pretend to treat the doll with their medical supplies.

Things to Talk About

- Have you ever heard an ambulance siren?
- Do you know why we need ambulances?

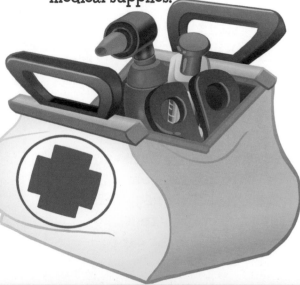

This is a good activity to do along with A Medical Play Kit (page 102).

Singing Fast and Slow

Help your child develop self-control and express feelings through music.

You'll Need

• Nothing

Things to Talk About

• Do all songs sound good when you sing them fast and slow?

• Which way do you like your favorite song?

Directions

1. Have your child choose one of their favorite songs to sing fast, then have them sing it slow.

2. Let your child sing several songs, then end with a slow one to help them settle down.

You might choose one of the songs in this book (page 276) for this activity.

This is my happy song, and I could sing it all day long!

Building Blocks

Get a head start on basic math, science and reading concepts.

Playing with Boats

Help your child develop creative play and learn more about their world.

You can make a second boat and have a race.

You'll Need

- Juice boxes
- Modeling dough or clay
- Straw or stick
- Paper (preferably tissue paper)

Directions

1. Cut off the front of an empty juice box and rinse it out. Have your child tear a piece of paper and attach it to a stick or straw to make a sail.

2. Place a bit of clay in the juicebox and stick in the straw to set up the sail.

3. Let your child sail the boat in a sink, bathtub or wide-bottomed pan.

Things to Talk About

- What happens when you blow on the sail?
- Does a piece of clay float if it's not in the boat?

Making Ice Pops

Help your child learn more about food.

You'll Need

- Small paper cups
- Ice pop sticks or plastic spoons
- Your favorite fruit juice
- Small pitcher

Directions

1. Set out some paper cups and pour the juice into a small pitcher or liquid measuring cup that your child can handle.

2. Let your child pour juice into the cups. Make sure they are not more than ¾ full.

3. Place the cups in the freezer. After 1 to 2 hours, when they are slushy but not frozen solid, take them out and let your child place ice pop sticks in the cups, making sure they stand straight up.

4. Let the ice pops freeze completely, at least 4 to 5 hours or up to overnight. Once frozen, tear off the cups and eat the ice pops.

Things to Talk About

- What did putting the juice in the freezer do to it?
- How long did it take?
- Why couldn't you put the ice pop sticks in the cups right away?

Looking for Letters

Help your child learn to look carefully and recognize symbols.

You'll Need

- Old magazines and newspapers
- Paper
- Glue or tape
- Scissors

Things to Talk About

- What is your favorite letter?
- What letters are in your name?
- Where else do you see letters?

Directions

1. If your child knows their letters, have them look through the magazines and newspapers for their favorite letters or the letters of their name. Younger children may be more interested in looking for animals, cars or airplanes.

2. Help your child cut out the letter they find and paste them on a piece of paper.

Go outside and look for letters on street signs and license plates.

Things That Are Round

Help your child learn about shapes and how to look carefully.

You'll Need

- Box with assorted round objects (such as paper plates, balls, rings, coins, etc.)
- Round scrap materials (buttons, paper circles, round stickers)
- Piece of paper for each child
- Round object to trace, like a cup
- Colored pencils or crayons
- Glue

Directions

1. Ask your child if they can think of anything that's round. Pull an object out of the box and show them. Let them feel the edges.

2. Give your child a piece of paper and show them how to trace circles from round objects. Let them play with the round scrap materials and make collages if they wish.

Things to Talk About

- Ask your child if they can think of other things that are round.
- Walk around the house and point out round things or go outside and look for them.
- Ask why certain things, such as car tires, are round.

Things That Are Alive

Help your child learn more about the world.

You'll Need

- Sheet of paper
- Old magazines
- Child-safe scissors
- Glue

Directions

1. Give your child a magazine. Ask them to cut out things in the magazine that are alive, and have the children paste them on a sheet of paper.

Things to Talk About

- What kinds of things are alive?
- Are plants alive?
- Is everything that grows alive?

Open and Closed

Help your child learn to use words.

You'll Need

- Box with a lid or a suitcase
- Blocks, toys or books

Directions

1. Show your child what the box or suitcase looks like when it's open and what it looks like when it's closed.

2. Let your child play with the box. Have them open it, fill it with toys, close it, then empty it again.

Things to Talk About

- What kinds of things open and close?
- What do they look like each way?
- Can you name things that open and close?
- Do your eyes and mouth open and close?
- What kinds of things can you find inside and outside that open and close?

Watching Seeds Grow

Help your child learn more about how things grow.

You'll Need

- 3 or 4 dried pinto beans
- Paper towels
- Glass jar
- Water

Directions

1. Line a jar with damp paper towels. Place three or four beans between the towels and the jar so you can see them. Put the jar in a sunny spot.

2. Add a little water to the bottom of the jar each day to keep the paper towel damp. Encourage your child to check for growth every day or so.

3. Once the plant is 2 inches tall, you can help your child plant it outdoors or in a pot.

Soaking the dried beans in water overnight will help them grow faster.

Things to Talk About

- What happens when plants grow?
- Do you see leaves and tiny blossoms?
- Why did we put the jar in a sunny place?

Big and Little

Help your child learn about sizes and practice working together.

You'll Need

- 2 baskets
- Assortment of blocks, boxes or plastic containers in 2 different sizes

Directions

1. Show your child the blocks. Ask them to show you a big block, then a little block.

2. Ask your child to make a tower just using the big blocks, then one using all the little blocks. What other ideas does your child have for using the blocks?

Things to Talk About

- What other things are big or little?
- Compare your hands to each other's and go around the house looking for other things that are big or little.

 You can also use plastic containers with lids or make blocks from milk cartons.

Sorting Buttons

Help your child recognize likeness and difference.

You'll Need

- Lots of buttons (some same, some different)
- Plastic containers or muffin tins
- Dishpan or shallow box

Directions

1. Place the buttons in a dishpan and let your child begin playing with them.

2. Give your child the plastic containers and encourage them to begin sorting the buttons. Help them decide if they want to sort them by color, size or amount of holes.

 For older children, do this activity with coins to start a discussion about money.

Things to Talk About

- How are the buttons different?
- How are they the same?

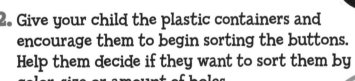

Measuring Time

Help your child learn more about time.

You'll Need

- Something that measures time (clock, stopwatch or phone timer)
- Paper
- Markers

Directions

1. Walk around your home and ask your child if they can point out different things that help us tell time, like a clock, phone, cable box, microwave, etc.

2. Using the paper and markers, help your child make a schedule that shows what time the same things happen each day. This could include the time they get up, when you leave for work, when they have lunch, etc.

Things to Talk About

- How do you know when it's time to get up?
- How long do you think it takes to read a story?

How Long?

Help your child develop curiosity and learn more about their world.

You may wish to show your child a real tape measure or ruler after this activity.

You'll Need

- Hands
- Feet
- String
- Block

Directions

1. Using their hands, feet, the string and the block, encourage your child to measure various things around your home. How many "hands" long is your table? What about in "feet"?

Things to Talk About

- Do you know how tall you are?
- Which is longer, your hand or your foot?

Comparing Weights

Help your child learn more about weights and measuring.

Your child might like to put their arms out and pretend to be a scale.

You'll Need

- Ruler
- Heavy string (6, 1-foot pieces)
- 2 paper cups
- Objects that can fit in the cups (beads, rubber bands, coins, small toys, blocks, etc.)

Directions

1. Make three holes under the lip of each cup and construct a simple scale by tying the strings through those holes, with the other ends tied together around the ends of the ruler.

2. Balance the ruler on your finger and let your child put some of the objects in each cup.

Things to Talk About

- What happens when you put things in the cup?
- Which object do you think is the heaviest?

A Look Inside

Help your child develop curiosity and learn more about their world.

You'll Need

- Something that can be taken apart (flashlight, old alarm clock, radio that doesn't work, etc.)
- Screwdriver

Directions

1. Have your child help you take apart something using a screwdriver. Examine all the pieces inside, then put it back together again.

You might also like to remind your child that people are all one piece.

Things to Talk About

- How do you think the object works?
- What would happen if you put it back differently from how you found it?

Say It Without Words

Help your child learn about different ways to communicate.

You'll Need

- Nothing

Remind your children there are lots of ways to communicate without speaking.

Directions

1. Say or do something and see if your child can find another way to communicate the same thing. For example, a hug can mean "I like you," shrugging your shoulders means "I don't know" and a wave can mean "Goodbye" or "Hello."

Things to Talk About

- How does a baby say they're hungry?
- How does a dog tell you it wants to go for a walk?

Pouring Water

Help your child learn more about comparisons and develop coordination.

You'll Need

- Small plastic pitcher
- Water
- Plastic containers of different sizes
- Towels
- Food coloring (optional)

Things to Talk About

- Which container has the most water? Which has the least?
- How can you tell?

This activity is best done outdoors.

Directions

1. See how well your child can pour water into the different-sized containers. For fun, you can color each container of water a different color.

Melting Ice Cubes

Help your child learn more about their world and practice waiting.

You'll Need

- Ice cube
- Small pan

Directions

1. Place an ice cube in a small pan and put it somewhere warm, like near a heating vent or in a sunny window. Ask your child what they think will happen to it. Wait about 10 minutes.

2. Talk about what happened. Is there a way to turn the water back into ice?

You might also like to do Making Ice Pops (page 113).

Things to Talk About

- What happens to snow and ice when it disappears?
- Explain how snow and ice are both really cold forms of water.

How Do Plants Eat?

Help your child learn more about foods and plants.

You'll Need

- Water
- Jar or glass
- Food coloring
- Celery stalks (including leaves)
- Peanut butter

Things to Talk About

- What makes plants grow?
- Do you know how they get food?

Directions

1. Cut about an inch from the bottom of a stalk of celery and show your child the veins in the stalk. Explain that the plant draws up water through these veins.

2. Place the celery stalk in a glass of water mixed with food coloring. In a few hours, the leaves will begin to turn the same color as the water. Cut the stalk again and you might be able to see colored veins.

3. Cut up the stalk and add peanut butter for a tasty, colorful snack.

Upside-Down Pictures

Help your child recognize likeness and difference.

You'll Need

- Paper
- Markers
- Toy cars or people

Directions

1. Show your child their toy, then turn it upside down. How does it look different? How does it look the same?

2. Give your child the paper and markers and encourage them to draw an upside-down scene.

Things to Talk About

- What if the world was upside down?
- Which direction would plants grow?
- What would happen when you dropped a ball?

A Close Look

Help your child develop curiosity and learn to look carefully.

You'll Need

- Magnifying glass
- Box of assorted objects (feathers, pine cones, thread, yarn, seeds, etc.)
- Newspaper or book

Directions

1. Show your child the magnifying glass. Let them use it to look at the newspaper— how do the letters and pictures look different?

2. Let your child use the magnifying glass to look at the different objects.

Things to Talk About

- What happens when you look through a magnifying glass?
- Do you notice things you didn't see before?

Your child might also like to look closely at carpet, hair or leaves.

Hard and Soft

Help your child recognize likeness and difference and develop their memory.

You'll Need

- Soft objects (cotton, handkerchief, tissue, stuffed animal, pot holder, etc.)
- Hard objects (block, wooden or metal toys, spoon, coin, crayon, etc.)
- Pillowcase

Directions

1. Take a walk around your home and see if your child can point out something that is hard and something that is soft.
2. Put all the objects in the pillowcase or another bag. Ask your child to put their hand in the bag and pull out something soft.
3. After they have done this, ask them to pull out something hard.

Things to Talk About

- Why are some things soft?
- Why are some things hard?

Safety First

Help your child learn about limits.

You'll Need

- Scissors
- Knives
- Forks
- Mirrors or other things made of glass

Things to Talk About

- Why do we have rules?
- What other rules are important to follow?

Directions

1. Have a talk with your child about important safety rules you have for these objects. You might include the following:

   - Never run while carrying scissors or other sharp objects.
   - Always return sharp things to their proper place.
   - Handle things made of glass carefully.
   - If glass breaks, don't try to pick up the pieces. Call a grownup for help.

You might like to make a list of rules to hang up.

An Eggshell Garden

Help your child develop self-control and learn more about growing.

You'll Need

- Eggshell halves
- Potting soil or dirt
- Packet of garden seeds
- Empty egg carton to hold shells
- Small plastic spoons
- Pitcher of water

Directions

1. Place the eggshell halves in the carton to keep them steady. Let your child fill the eggshells with potting soil. Small plastic spoons will make this easier.

2. Show your child how to plant a seed in each shell. Water according to the seed instructions.

3. When the plants grow to a few inches, you can plant them outside, shells and all.

Things to Talk About

- Why do we water the seeds?
- What else do plants need to grow?

Remind your child that eggshells are delicate and to be very careful.

Mixing Colors

Help your child learn more about their world and develop healthy curiosity.

💡 Repeat this activity to let your child see different color combinations.

You'll Need

- Jar
- Food coloring (4 colors)
- Water
- Newspaper or plastic covering
- Spoon or ice pop stick

Directions

1. Lay down newspaper or a plastic covering to protect your workspace from stains.

2. Give your child a half-full jar of water and a spoon. Let them choose a color and add a few drops to their water. Encourage your child to watch it spread for a bit, then stir it in.

3. Let your child choose a second color to mix with the first.

Things to Talk About

- What happens when you mix the two colors?
- How much food coloring does it take to color a whole jar of water?

Occupations

Help your child learn more about work and develop their imagination.

You'll Need

- Nothing

Directions

1. Explain that an "occupation" is the kind of work that a person does. Ask your child to think of jobs that grownups do, such as mail-carrier, cook, teacher or doctor.

2. Choose one of the jobs to act out and see if your child can guess what you are doing. Once they guess, see if your child would like to act out a job too.

Things to Talk About

- Why do people have jobs?
- What job would you like to have when you grow up?

Caution

Help your child learn about limits.

You'll Need

- Paper
- Marker
- Tape

Directions

1. Ask your child to think of things that can be dangerous. This might include the oven, a heavy door, a swing set, etc.

2. Help your child make small signs that say "caution" to tape on these objects.

Remind your child that "caution" means they need to be very careful when they are near those objects.

Things to Talk About

- Why do we need to be careful around these objects?

Loud and Quiet

Help your child develop self-control and use play to work on feelings.

You'll Need

- Metal pans
- Wooden spoons

Things to Talk About

- Can you think of sounds that are scary?
- Are any sounds happy or sad?

Directions

1. Let your child play with the spoons and pan. Can they use the spoons to make quiet noises? What about loud ones? Which is easier to make?

2. Ask your child if they can make loud noises and quiet noises with their voices too.

After you are done playing with the pots and pans, sing "Clean Up, Pick Up, Put Away" (page 276).

Grandparents Day

Help your child learn more about their world.

You'll Need

- Paper
- Markers

Things to Talk About

- Even though some people don't know their grandparents, everybody has them.

Directions

1. If you can, share something with your child that came from one of your grandparents. It might be a picture, object, song or game.

2. Talk to your child about their grandparents, if you can. Do they have any objects from them, or did their grandparents teach them a game or song?

3. Draw a simple family tree that shows your child, you and any other parents and all the grandparents your child has.

Alike and Different

Help your child recognize likeness and difference.

You'll Need

- Nothing

Directions

1. Ask your child to think about their friends, siblings or cousins. Can they think of some ways they are alike? They might live near one another, like to do the same things, like the same snacks, etc.

2. Now see if they can think of things that are different. They might have different families, wear different clothes, have different colors of hair or skin, etc.

Things to Talk About

- Is anyone else exactly the same as you? Why not?

Things That Are Fragile

Help your child develop creative play.

You'll Need

- Pipe cleaners

💡 **Remind your child that some broken things can be repaired, but some are too hard to put back together again.**

Directions

1. Give your child a few pipe cleaners and let them make a pretend object. They might like to make a person, spider or something else entirely.

2. Ask your child to pretend their pipe cleaner sculpture is made of glass. How would they pass it to you?

Things to Talk About

- What happens to your sculpture if you don't handle it carefully?
- Is it easy to bend out of shape?

Talking About Disabilities

Help your child understand and accept individual differences.

You'll Need

- Nothing

Things to Talk About

- Discuss how using crutches or wheelchairs takes practice, and these people who use them can feel proud of using them well.

Directions

1. Has your child ever seen someone using a wheelchair or wearing leg or arm braces? Why do they think some people need those?

2. Explain that people use these things to make it easier to get around. Hearing aids and guide dogs or canes can also help people do things more easily.

3. Let your child know people who have disabilities became that way because of an illness or an accident, not because they saw, heard or did something bad.

131

Sorting Shapes

Help your child recognize likeness and difference.

You'll Need

- Set of cardboard or heavy paper shapes (circles, squares and triangles in different colors and sizes)

- Shoeboxes or small containers

Directions

1. Spread the shapes out on a table or floor where your child can play with them.

2. Ask your child to find the shapes that are alike. Your child might choose to sort by color, size or shape.

Keep the shapes in one of the boxes to use again.

Things to Talk About

- How are the objects that you've put together alike?

- How are they different?

What Do You Call Me?

Help your child learn more about their world.

You'll Need

- Nothing

Things to Talk About

- Can a person have a few different names?

- Do you have any nicknames?

Directions

1. Ask your child what they call you. Have they ever heard anyone call you something else? Do they also know what other adults call you?

2. Talk about another person that has a few different names. For example, the Ruler of the Neighborhood of Make-Believe is King Friday, but Prince Wednesday calls him Dad.

What Do You Hear?

Help your child learn to listen carefully.

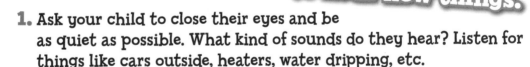 **Repeat this activity in different places to hear new things.**

You'll Need

- Ball

Directions

1. Ask your child to close their eyes and be as quiet as possible. What kind of sounds do they hear? Listen for things like cars outside, heaters, water dripping, etc.

2. With their eyes closed, make a specific sound for your child to identify, like snapping your fingers, tapping your foot, bouncing a ball, etc.

Things to Talk About

- Is it hard to listen carefully?

- Can you hear as well when you're doing something else?

Modeling Dough Letters

Help your child recognize and use letters.

You'll Need

- Modeling dough, like Play-Doh®

Directions

1. Give your child time to play with the dough—encourage them to knead, poke, punch and roll it.

2. Show your child how to roll out pieces of the dough to make long strands. Can your child loop and shape the strands to make different letters?

Things to Talk About

- Do you know the alphabet?

- How can you turn a "C" into an "O"?

 **Very young children might like to make animals instead.**

Lip-Reading

Help your child learn about different ways people communicate.

You'll Need

- Nothing

Show your child a video of people using sign language.

Directions

1. Have your child try to read your lips while you say a few simple sentences without using your voice, like "How are you?" and "I love you."

2. Repeat the same sentences out loud, then have your child try to read your lips again.

Things to Talk About

- How do you feel when you can't understand me?
- How would you feel if you couldn't hear at all?

Making Signs

Help your child recognize and use symbols and learn more about their world.

You'll Need

- Notecards or strips of paper
- Markers or crayons
- Tape

Directions

1. Ask your child to look around the room and name the things they see. As they do so, write the word on a card and have your child tape it to the object.

2. Leave the cards up for a while so your child can practice "reading" the words.

Things to Talk About

- What do we use signs for?
- Where else do you see signs?

On a nice day, take a walk and point out other signs.

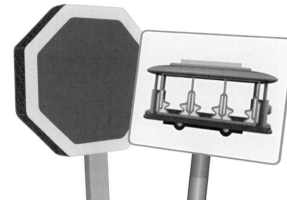

Going Down the Drain

Help your child use play to work on feelings.

You'll Need

- Colander
- Sand
- Water
- Small plastic toys
- Dishpan

Directions

1. Show your child how sand easily passes through the colander. Let your child push some sand through the colander, keeping it over a dishpan to catch the sand.

2. Place the toys in the colander and let your child pour water over them.

This is a good outdoor activity.

Things to Talk About

- Did the water go through?
- What about the toys?
- Why does sand go through the colander but not your fingers?

Getting Permission

Help your child learn more about their world and more about work.

You'll Need

- Driver's license
- Homemade "tricycle license"
- Tricycle

Directions

1. Show your child your driver's license and explain that it gives you permission to drive a car. Can your child think of other things that require a license, like working as a doctor or flying a plane?

2. Ask your child if they would like to get their "tricycle license." Have them show you they can get on a tricycle, ride forward, stop and carefully get off.

Things to Talk About

- Why do we need permission to do some things?
- What else do you ask permission for?

Talking About School

Help your child use play to work on feelings.

You'll Need

- Pictures of things you would find in a school
- Large piece of paper or cardboard
- Glue

Directions

1. Ask your child what they think children do at school. Do they know anyone who goes to school?

2. Show your child the pictures of school things. Do they know what the object is or how students would use it?

Things to Talk About

- Some children might be afraid to go to school for the first time.
- Can you think of other things you did for the first time?

Visits

Help your child develop their imagination.

You'll Need

• Nothing

Directions

1. Tell your child about a special visit you remember taking, perhaps to a family member or friend's home. Tell your child how long you were gone and what you did while you were there.

2. Encourage your child to pretend about going somewhere for a visit. If they could visit anywhere or anyone, what would they do?

If you can, take your child on a short trip to see a friend or neighbor.

Things to Talk About

• Where are you going?

• Who will you see?

• When will you be coming home?

Making Up Poems

Help your child learn to use words and express feelings in appropriate ways.

You'll Need

- Paper
- Pencil, pen or marker
- Children's poems, from a book or online

Things to Talk About

- Do you know what a rhyme is?
- Do you like reading poems?

Directions

1. Choose a short poem or nursery rhyme to read to your child.

2. Play a rhyming game in which you say a simple word and your child comes up with as many rhymes as they can.

3. Help your child make up a simple poem with rhyming words.

Out of Energy

Help your child learn more about their world.

Your child might like to go around the house and point out which things need electricity.

You'll Need

- Flashlight
- New batteries
- Old, worn-out batteries

Directions

1. Ask your child if they have ever used a toy or controller that needed a new battery. What happened?

2. If you have a flashlight and some old batteries, you might be able to show them the difference in the amount of light the worn-out batteries produce compared to new ones.

Things to Talk About

- Can you remember a time when your whole house lost power?
- What sorts of things can you do without electricity?

You Look Different

Help your child recognize likeness and difference.

You'll Need

- Hat, scarf or bandana
- Mirror
- Dress-up clothes
- Sunglasses

Things to Talk About

- Does changing what you're wearing make you look different?
- Does it make you different on the inside?

Directions

1. Let your child watch as you use a hat, scarf or bandana to cover your hair and put on sunglasses. Can they still tell who you are?

2. Encourage your child to put the sunglasses and scarf on a doll or stuffed animal, and to play with the dress-up clothes themselves. Let them see how different they look in a mirror. Remember, "You can change your hair or what you wear, but no matter what you do, you're still you."

Which Is Which?

Help your child learn to listen carefully.

You'll Need

- Spoon
- Piece of wood
- Metal pan
- Two glasses, one filled with water

Directions

1. Encourage your child to listen carefully as you clap your hands and then knock on wood. Can they tell the difference between the two sounds? Have them turn around while you do it again. Can they tell you which is which?

2. Repeat the activity by tapping the spoon on the wood and then the metal, and then again with the empty and full water glasses.

Things to Talk About

- Can you tell what's happening without using your eyes?
- Why is it important to listen carefully?

People and Machines

Help your child learn more about their world.

You'll Need

- Flashlight
- Vacuum cleaner
- Light switch
- Television

Directions

1. Ask your child if they can tell you some ways people and machines are different. You can suggest that people eat food and machines don't; people have feelings and machines don't; or that people can think on their own but machines can't.

2. Open a flashlight to show your child the batteries, then let them turn it on and off with the switch. Point out that your child is the one who is making the machine work.

Things to Talk About

- What other things have switches?
- Do you have an on-off switch?

141

Safety Rules

Help your child learn about limits.

You'll Need

- Large piece of paper, like a cut-open paper grocery bag
- Marker

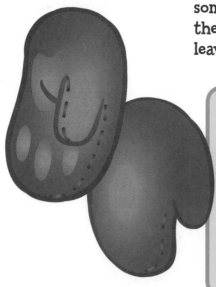

Directions

1. Can your child think of some rules that you have to make sure they stay safe? This might include wearing a seatbelt in the car, putting on sunblock at the beach or pool, wearing boots, a hat and mittens when it's cold, etc.

2. What are some safety rules that mean a person must not do something? Come up with some with your child and write them on the piece of paper. This might include not touching the stove, not leaving the yard without permission, not running in the house, etc.

Things to Talk About

- Why do we need to follow rules?
- Are there any rules that you find difficult to follow?

Remind your child to "Stop and listen to stay safe."

Same But Different

Help your child learn about comparisons.

You'll Need

- Book with pictures of different kinds of birds

You can do this activity with any kind of animal.

Directions

1. Look through the book with your child. Can they point out what is similar about all the birds? What makes them different?

Things to Talk About

- What do all birds have in common?
- Are all birds the same size or the same color?

Looking for Numbers

Help your child recognize and use symbols.

Your child might like to practice counting the things around them.

You'll Need

- Old calendar pages
- Scissors

Directions

1. Show your child the old calendar pages and help them cut out the numbers into individual squares.

2. Let your child play with the number squares. If you'd like, use them like flashcards and see if your child can name each number.

Things to Talk About

- How high can you count?
- Do you have a favorite number?

All About Baskets

Help your child recognize likeness and difference.

You'll Need

- Baskets in assorted shapes and sizes

Directions

1. Show your child the different baskets. How are they alike? How are they different?

2. Help your child come up with a few ideas for using the baskets in different ways. You may like to serve a snack in one, use another as the goal for a toss game, make up a story about the basket, etc.

Things to Talk About

- Are some of the baskets better suited to some uses than others?

Explain that no two baskets are exactly alike, just like people.

Card Sorting

Help your child recognize and use symbols.

You'll Need

- Deck of cards

Toddlers may just enjoy the feel of the cards.

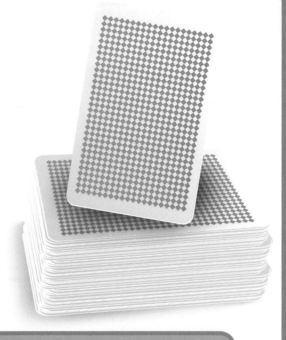

Directions

1. Show your child a deck of cards. If they're old enough, they might recognize the numbers on them.

2. Have your child sort the cards in different ways. They can make piles according to numbers, colors or shapes (suits).

Things to Talk About

- What do all the cards have in common?
- Can you make a set of cards from 1 to 10?

Mechanical Monsters

Help your child learn more about their world and use play to work on feelings.

You'll Need

- Magazine or catalog pictures of trucks and construction equipment
- Scissors
- Toy trucks and diggers

Things to Talk About

- Remind your child that people make the machines go.

Directions

1. Help your child look through the magazine for pictures of construction equipment (or print some from a computer). Tell your child the specific names of different equipment and what they are used for. You might want to borrow a children's book about trucks and diggers from your library for this activity.

2. If you have toy trucks, take them out for play.

If you can, visit a construction site to see the machines.

Exercise Every Day

Help your child develop muscle control.

You'll Need

• Nothing

💡 **If you can, have organized exercise with your child every day.**

Directions

1. Set aside a few minutes to do organized exercises with your child.

2. Together with your child, stand in place with your legs slightly apart and put your hands on your hips and twist from side to side. You can also stretch out your arms in front of you and pretend to swim.

3. Lie on the floor with your legs straight, then open and close them in a scissor fashion. You can also keep your legs straight and your arms at your sides and roll to one side and then to the other.

Things to Talk About

• Do you like to exercise?

• Why is exercising good for you?

Let's Make a Zoo

Help your child develop creative play and coordination.

You can also use Animal Blocks for this activity (page 47).

You'll Need

- Set of blocks or boxes
- Toy animals
- Toy people

Directions

1. Help your child make a pretend zoo. Using the blocks or boxes, they can section off different kinds of toy animals.

2. If they'd like, they can have toy people go to their zoo and enjoy seeing the different exhibits they set up.

Things to Talk About

- What animals do you see at a zoo?
- Why do zoo animals need to be separated from one another?

Using Silverware

Help your child learn more about foods and learn to do things independently.

You'll Need

- Spoons, forks and butter knives
- Food you eat with a spoon (yogurt, applesauce, etc.)
- Food you eat with a fork (chunky vegetables or protein)
- Bread
- Soft butter or other spread
- Plates, bowls, etc.

Directions

1. This is a snack or mealtime activity. Your child is probably used to using a spoon, but they may need more practice with a fork.

2. You can also let your child practice spreading using a butter knife. Lightly toasting the bread will make it less likely to tear.

Things to Talk About

- Why do we need different utensils?
- What do we use knives for?

Humming a Song

Help your child express feelings through music and learn to listen carefully.

You'll Need

- Music

Directions

1. See if your child can practice humming along with some music.

2. Now, without the help of background music, you and your child could try humming a familiar song. (It could even be as familiar as "Happy Birthday.")

3. If you'd like, turn this into a game by humming a small portion of a song and seeing if your child can guess what it is.

Things to Talk About

- What other songs do you know?

- Do you have a favorite song?

If your child can't guess the song you're humming, sing a word or two to help them guess.

Mail a Letter

Help your child learn more about the world and learn more about money.

You'll Need

- Paper
- Markers and pens
- Envelopes
- Stamps

Directions

1. Would your child like to mail a letter to a family member or friend? Give them a piece of paper for a small drawing and then let them dictate the words they would like to say.

2. When the letter is finished, help your child put it into an envelope and seal it. Then show your child how you address and stamp the envelope.

Things to Talk About

- Why do we need to put a stamp on the envelope?
- Why is it important to know someone's address when you want to mail something to them?

Your child might like putting the envelope in your mailbox.

A Shopping List

Help your child practice making choices.

You'll Need

- Paper
- Pen

Directions

1. Using paper and a pen, list the days of the week and have your child help you come up with a snack idea for each day.

2. Explain that you might not be able to get everything on the list, but you can make choices that include a variety of foods.

3. Once the menus are finished, make a shopping list of all the things you need to make all the snacks. Have your child help you check to see if you already have any of the ingredients at home.

Things to Talk About

- Why is it helpful to make a list?
- Why did we check to see if we already had things on the list?

Thunder Noises

Help your child use play to work on feelings.

💡 Think of a signal before you start so your child knows when to stop.

You'll Need

- Metal pans
- Wooden spoons
- Flashlight (optional)

Directions

1. Let your child bang the pans with wooden spoons to make "thunder sounds." You could also darken the room and turn a flashlight on and off to make lightning.

2. See if your child can make different kinds of "thunder" noises by banging at different speeds.

Things to Talk About

- What kinds of things can you do if you're afraid in a thunderstorm?
- Do thunder and lightning keep going on when the storm is over?

Many Ways

Help your child understand and accept individual differences.

You'll Need

• Scarves

This is a good activity for a group.

Directions

1. Talk to your child about how people have different ideas about using things and how we don't have to do everything the way someone else does it.

2. Give your child a scarf and have them come up with a few different ways to use it.

Things to Talk About

• Can you use the scarf as a streamer? To play peekaboo? To hide toys?

• What else can you do with it?

What is Adoption?

Help your child feel comfortable asking questions and learn different ways people communicate.

You'll Need

• Nothing

Things to Talk About

• What are some ways family members show they love one another?

Directions

1. Has your child ever heard of adoption? Explain that all babies are born in the same way but if birth parents aren't able to care for a child, they can find other parents to give the baby the love and care it needs.

2. See if your child has any questions about adoption. Reassure them that adoptive families love one another the same way other families do.

Connect the Stars

Help your child develop muscle control and learn more about stars.

You'll Need

- Plain paper
- Markers or crayons
- Foil stars (optional)

Directions

1. Use stars instead of dots to create a design on a piece of paper. You might choose a simple shape like a square or the first initial of your child's name.

2. Show your child how to complete the design by drawing lines to connect the stars.

Things to Talk About

- Do you know what a constellation is?
- What do you see when you look up at the night sky?

You can also place the stars randomly and let your child make their own design.

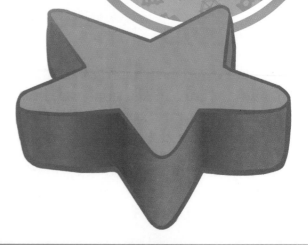

Things that Spin

Help your child learn more about the world and develop creative play.

You'll Need

- Tops
- Coins
- Pencils
- Spoons

Things to Talk About

- What else could you spin?
- Do some things spin better than others?

Directions

1. Show your child how to spin a top. Let them practice making it spin for as long as they can.

2. Come up with a few other things that you could make spin. For example, coins, spoons and pencils.

Now You See It, Now You Don't

Help your child develop healthy curiosity.

Show your child the tiny pieces of eraser that are left on the paper.

You'll Need

- Erasers
- Pencils
- Pen
- Paper

Directions

1. Give your child the materials to play with and let them play around with them, making marks and then erasing them.

2. Make a few pen marks. Can the eraser make them disappear?

Things to Talk About

- Can you erase markers or paint?
- Where do the pencil marks go when you erase them?

Shadow Dancers

Help your child express feelings through movement and dance.

You'll Need

- Large white sheet
- Flashlight or high intensity lamp
- Familiar toys

Directions

1. Hang the sheet from a doorway and shine a bright light behind it. With your child standing on the opposite side of the light, show them how standing in front of the light makes a shadow on the sheet.

2. Let your child make their own shadow dancer by dancing between the light and the sheet (you may wish to record this to show them afterward).

This is a good group activity.

Things to Talk About

- What makes a shadow?
- How is a shadow different from the real thing?

A New Language

Help your child learn to listen carefully and learn different ways people communicate.

You'll Need

- Globe or map of the world

Things to Talk About

- What would you do if you could not understand the language a person was using?
- How else could you communicate?

Directions

1. Show your child the map or globe and point to a country that doesn't speak English as a first language. Do you know what language the people there speak?

2. Look up a video of people speaking a language other than English. See if you can memorize a few simple phrases from a new language.

You might like to take out a phrase book in another language from your library.

Let's Explore

Help your child learn more about nature.

You'll Need

- Masking tape
- Paper bags
- Sticks

Things to Talk About

- What clues help you identify each object without seeing it?

Directions

1. Take a nature walk around your neighborhood or local park and gather interesting things in a paper bag along the way, like fallen leaves, small stones, acorns or feathers.

2. When you get home, see if your child can identify the different objects in their bag just by feeling them.

3. If you'd like, use masking tape to hang the lighter objects from a stick to make a simple mobile.

You can also play this game with small toys or household objects.

What's Under the Bandage?

Help your child learn more about body parts and develop creative play.

You'll Need

- An old sheet or pillowcase
- Scissors

Directions

1. Cut the old pillowcase or sheet into long strips about 3 inches wide and 2 to 3 feet long.

2. Wrap a strip of cloth around your own arm like a bandage. Let your child unwind it to see that your arm is still underneath.

3. Wrap your child's arm, knee or foot with the bandage and let them unwind it when they're done pretending.

Pretend bandages can reassure children that bandages don't change what's underneath.

Things to Talk About

- Why do we need bandages sometimes?
- Can you name all your body parts?

Parental Care

Help your child try out different roles.

You'll Need

- Stuffed animal

Directions

1. If you can, tell your child about some of the ways your parents—their grandparents—cared for you.

2. Talk about some of the other ways parents care for their children. You might list things like tucking their kids in at night, preparing meals or bandaging a cut.

3. See if your child would like to pretend to be a parent to their stuffed animal.

Things to Talk About

- Lots of people take care of kids, like grandparents, aunts, uncles and friends.

A Cardboard Mouth

Help your child use play to work on feelings.

You'll Need

- Several pieces of lightweight cardboard, like from cereal boxes

Directions

1. Cut a piece of cardboard into a 3-by-5-inch piece and fold it in half to make a pretend mouth.

2. Let your child play with the card and see what they do with it. If they haven't already done so, ask them to pretend the card is a mouth.

Things to Talk About

- What kinds of things can we do with our mouths? Eating, singing, yawning and whistling are a few examples.

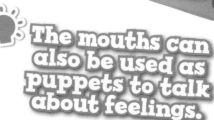

The mouths can also be used as puppets to talk about feelings.

157

After the field trip is over, have your child make a drawing of their favorite moment.

A Neighborhood Field Trip

Help your child learn more about their community.

You'll Need

- Paper
- Pen or pencil

Directions

1. Plan a field trip around your neighborhood. Make a list of places you can visit, like the grocery store, a playground, the library, etc.

Things to Talk About

- Is it possible to visit everywhere in just one day?
- What will you do for lunch and snacks?

Flashlight Power

Help your child develop curiosity and their imagination.

You'll Need

- Flashlights

Things to Talk About

- How do you feel when you are in the dark?
- Does having a flashlight change how you feel?

Directions

1. Partially close any curtains or blinds and dim the lights to darken the room you are in. Let your child use the flashlight to "explore" the room.

2. Come up with a few fun ways to use flashlights. You can make shadow puppets, play flashlight tag or invent a new game.

 **Remind your child not to shine the light in anyone's eyes.**

Water Science

Help your child learn more about floating, evaporation and more.

You'll Need

- Clear glass or plastic bowls
- Water
- Food coloring
- Cooking utensils
- Toy boat or other floating objects
- Dry-erase marker

Directions

1. Fill the bowl halfway with water and help your child experiment with some basic scientific principles. They can see which objects float, how food coloring slowly disperses throughout the water, how the colors combine to make new ones and how stirring water makes currents and swirls.

2. When you're done playing, use a dry-erase marker to note the level of the water. Leave the bowl out for several days—what happens?

Things to Talk About

- Does everything float?
- What color combinations can you make?
- Does the water change color all at once?

Growing Up

Develop the skills needed for growing up on the inside.

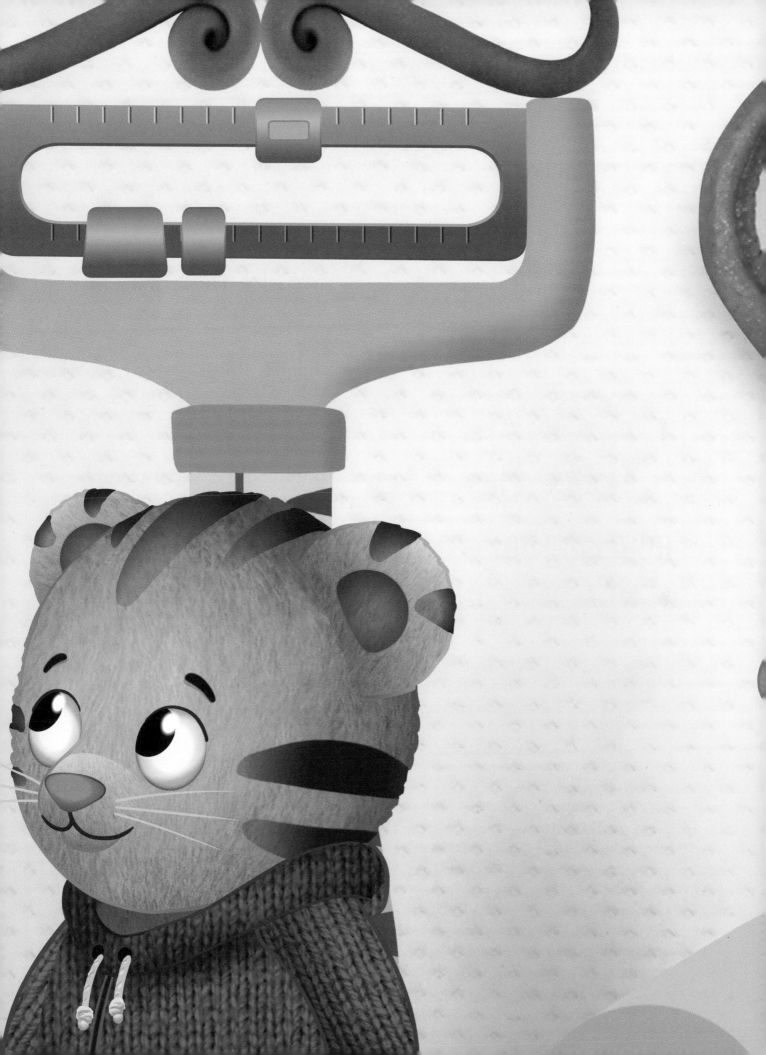

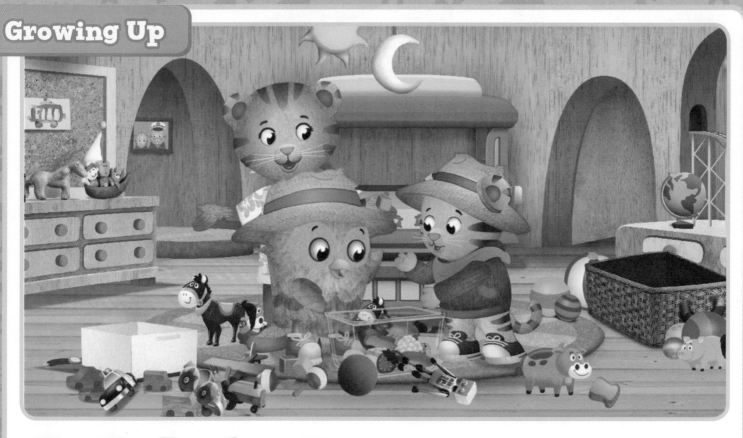

A Job to Do

Help your child learn to do things independently and practice making choices.

You'll Need

- Large piece of paper or cardboard
- Name tags
- Tape

Directions

1. On the paper, list some jobs or chores that need to be done regularly, such as putting away toys, watering plants, sweeping, etc.

2. Write the names of each person who lives in your home on separate name tags. Help your child pick a chore they would like to do and tape their name next to it.

Things to Talk About

- Why is it important to do jobs?
- Do you know what responsibility means?

You can switch around who does each chore every week.

You've Got to Do It

Help your child learn the difference between real and pretend and develop the ability to keep on trying.

You'll Need

- "Magic wand" (pencil, stick, etc.)
- Puzzle

Directions

1. Have your child wish the puzzle was put together. Wave the wand and see what happens!

2. Ask your child if the puzzle was really put together. Then encourage your child to complete the puzzle on their own.

Things to Talk About

- Have you ever wished something would happen by magic?
- What kinds of things?

Help the task seem easier by flipping all the puzzle pieces right side up.

Someplace Else

Help your child learn self-control.

You'll Need

- Nothing

Directions

1. Have a conversation with your child about coming up with other things to do when they aren't allowed to do what they want. Help your child think of places where they can play noisy games, or make a list of quiet games they can play.

Things to Talk About

- What is a quiet or "inside" voice?
- Why can't we always do noisy things?
- Is there a special place to use loud toys?

All By Myself

Help your child feel proud of their accomplishments.

You'll Need

- Your child's coat or jacket
- Other clothing (shoes, belts, skirts, etc.)

Directions

1. **Ask your child to think of things they can do by themselves. Can they walk up stairs or button a sweater?**

2. Let your child practice putting on clothes by themself. Lay the open jacket on the floor upside down so the neck part is closest to your child. Show your child how to put their arms in the sleeves and lift the coat over their heads so the jacket is right side up again.

3. If your child already knows how to put on their own coat, show them how to tie or buckle a shoe.

Things to Talk About

- If this is your child's first time trying one of these things, their attempt won't be perfect.
- Talk about how new skills take practice and point out the things they did well.

Make Your Own Choice

Help your child practice making choices.

Remind your child there are some things we all have to do, whether we like them or not.

You'll Need

- Dress-up clothes
- Crayons or markers
- Books
- Trucks and cars

Directions

1. Suggest a few different activities and let your child decide which one they would like to do. They can play dress-up for a pretend party, color, look through books or play with trucks and cars.

Things to Talk About

- Do you like making your own choices?
- Do you always get to make your own choices about what to do?

Lacing Shoes

Help your child develop coordination and learn to do things independently.

You'll Need

- Pair of shoes with laces

Directions

1. Pull the laces out of the shoes and let your child practice threading the laces back through the holes. It might frustrate them at first, but encourage them to keep trying.

2. If your child is old enough, you can show them how to tie the shoes and practice doing that too.

Things to Talk About

- Was it easy or hard to thread the laces through the holes?
- Did it get easier the more you practiced?

If the lace ends are frayed, wrap them with tape to make this easier.

Hairstyles

Help your child develop their imagination and use play to work on feelings.

You'll Need

- Hair rollers
- Barrettes
- Comb
- Brush
- Water
- Mirror
- Dolls with hair (optional)

Directions

1. Use the hair products to temporarily give your child a new hairstyle. They might enjoy seeing their hair in rollers or adding different barrettes.

2. You can also use the comb to make a new part. Adding a little water may help with this if their hair is very short.

> If your child doesn't want to change their hair, they might like doing this on a doll.

Things to Talk About

- Do you like your new hairstyle?
- Does changing your hair change who you are on the inside?

I'm Taking Care of You

Help your child try out different roles.

You'll Need

- Dolls or stuffed animals
- Plants (optional)

Things to Talk About

- Do you have anything you take care of?
- Who takes care of you?

Directions

1. Talk about how plants need light, water and soil to stay alive. House plants need someone to take care of them. If you have a plant, show your child how you water it to take care of it.

2. Let your child pick out a doll or stuffed animal and pretend it's their pet or a baby they need to take care of. What kinds of things do they need to do for it?

Learning to Do New Things

Help your child feel proud of their accomplishments.

You'll Need

- Large piece of paper
- Marker

Directions

1. Make a list on the paper of things your child has recently learned to do. This might include walking down stairs alone, putting on a jacket, tying shoes, remembering to brush teeth before bed, etc.

2. As your child learns more new skills, go back to this list and add to it.

Things to Talk About

- What other things do you want to learn?

Remind your child they are growing inside as well as out.

167

Practicing

Help your child practice new skills and making choices.

You'll Need

- Nothing

Things to Talk About

- How long do you think it will take to learn your new skill?

- What do you want to practice after that?

Directions

1. If you have a special skill, like playing an instrument, doing a handstand or baking or drawing, tell your child about it. Tell them how long it took to learn and about a time when you were frustrated while practicing.

2. Can your child remember how it felt the last time they were practicing a new skill? How did they feel after they learned it?

3. Pick a new skill to practice. Younger children could practice things like pouring from a pitcher or going up and down stairs, while older children may want to practice tying shoes or riding a bike.

You might want to sing "Keep Trying" (page 279) after this conversation.

Take Care of Your Teeth

Help your child learn more about their body and foods.

You'll Need

- Paper
- Pictures of nutritious food
- Glue

Directions

1. Can your child remember the last time they were at the dentist? Ask if they remember the examination and having their teeth cleaned.

2. What foods are good for your teeth? What foods are not good for your teeth? If you'd like, have your child glue pictures of nutritious food on a piece of paper and hang it on your refrigerator.

Apples, carrots and leafy greens are all good for your teeth.

Things to Talk About

- Do you think these foods are good for the rest of your body too?
- How do you feel when you have too many sweets or salty foods?

Brushing Your Teeth

Help your child learn to do things independently.

You'll Need

- Toothpaste
- Toothbrush
- Floss
- Mirror

Directions

1. After meal and snack times, have your child practice brushing their teeth. Your child might be more interested in this if you make homemade toothpaste (recipe on following page).

2. You can also show your child how to floss their teeth.

Things to Talk About

- Does your mouth feel different before and after you brush?
- Why is brushing important?

Making Toothpaste

Help your child learn to take care of themself.

You'll Need

- 4 tsp baking soda
- 1 tsp salt
- 1 tsp flavoring (vanilla, almond or peppermint extract)
- Toothbrush
- Floss
- Airtight containers

Directions

1. Add all the ingredients to a small airtight container and mix them together. Next time your child needs to brush their teeth, have them use the homemade toothpaste.

Remind your child that strong teeth look nice and help you eat.

Things to Talk About

- When do we brush our teeth?
- How else do you take care of your teeth?

Things I Can Do

Help your child understand and accept individual differences and feel proud of their accomplishments.

You'll Need

- Nothing

Things to Talk About

- Do you feel proud of yourself?
- Are you better at some things than others?

Directions

1. Ask your child to think of some things they like doing and that they think they do well. This might include catching a ball, cleaning up, following directions, drawing pictures, etc.

2. Remind your child that they weren't always able to do these things!

 If doing this with a group, point out how each kid has something they are very good at.

Ways I Am Growing

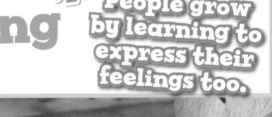 People grow by learning to express their feelings too.

Help your child learn more about growing.

You'll Need

- Baby pictures of your child
- Pictures of yourself growing up

Directions

1. Show your child the pictures of both them and you as a baby (and pictures of yourself growing up, if you have them).

2. Ask your child how tall they think they will be when they are done growing and what special skills they want to have.

Things to Talk About

- What kinds of things can you do now that you couldn't when you were a baby?

171

💡 **Remind your child that everybody can do something.**

Children Can

Help your child feel proud of the things they are able to do right now.

You'll Need

- Nothing

Directions

1. Start this activity by singing "Everybody Is Big Enough to Do Something" (page 280) and acting out some of the words.

2. Ask your child to think of some things they can do that a bigger person would have trouble doing. This might include sitting under a table, playing all day or climbing a jungle gym.

Things to Talk About

- What are some things people can't learn to do?

- Do you like to pretend to do these things, like flying by yourself?

Washing Toys

Help your child learn to do take care of their belongings.

You'll Need

- Plastic bowls or buckets
- Soapy water
- Cloths or sponges
- Old toothbrushes, nail brushes or scrub brushes
- Washable toys
- Towel

Directions

1. If the weather is nice, this could be done outdoors. Otherwise this should be set up in a bathtub.

2. Add warm water to the bowl or bucket and let your child add some soap and mix it up. Show them how to scrub their (washable) toys, then rinse them clean.

3. Have your child dry their toys with a towel, then put them away.

Things to Talk About
- Why do we need to clean our things?
- Does it feel nice to wear clean clothes and play with clean toys?

My History

Help your child learn more about their world and understand and accept individual differences.

You'll Need

- Paper
- Stapler
- Scissors
- Tape
- Glue
- Magazine pictures of babies, baby toys and baby clothes

You can also include favorite foods, colors and animals.

Directions

1. Make a "history" book for your child by stapling several blank pages together.

2. Include information such as your child's date of birth, city of birth, a family tree and baby pictures. Encourage your child to cut out and glue in pictures of baby clothes and toys.

Things to Talk About
- What is your earliest memory?
- Do you have any favorite memories from growing up?

Setting the Table

Help your child learn new responsibilities.

You'll Need

- Placemats
- Plates or bowls
- Silverware
- Cups
- Napkins

Directions

1. Help your child get started by giving them the correct number of placemats or arranging the exact amount of chairs around the table.

2. Let your child set the table on their own. Challenge them to make each place setting look the same, with the silverware, cups and napkins in the same place.

If you don't have plastic dishes for this activity, you may want to make a set out of cardboard.

Things to Talk About

- What things do you need to set the table for a meal?
- Do you always need spoons and knives?

Trying on Clothes

Help your child use play to work on feelings.

You'll Need

- Dresses
- Shirts
- Ties
- Shoes
- Hats
- Mirror

If your child wears any hand-me-down clothes, ask them how they feel about that.

Things to Talk About

- What happens to your clothes after you grow out of them?
- Would it be fun if your clothes could grow along with you?

Directions

1. Let your child try on different combinations of clothes and then look in the mirror.

2. Ask your child if they think they look different in the dress-up clothes. Do they feel like someone else?

Buttoning

Help your child develop muscle control and the ability to keep trying.

You'll Need

- Clothing that fastens with buttons, like a shirt

Things to Talk About

- How many buttons are on each piece of clothing?
- In what other ways do we fasten clothing?

Directions

1. Let your child practice buttoning and unbuttoning an item of clothing.

2. If you have a piece of clothing with larger or smaller buttons, let your child try buttoning that as well.

The Best of Whatever You Are

Help your child feel proud of their accomplishments and accept individual differences.

You'll Need

- Nothing

Directions

1. Explain to your child that every person is special and can be the "best" of something.

2. Ask your child to think of things that they can do well. This might include:
   - Sharing
   - Running, hopping or skipping
   - Zipping a jacket or putting on a coat
   - Singing a song, painting a picture, dancing to music

Things to Talk About

- Can you demonstrate something that you do well?

- How do you feel when you do something you're good at?

Remind your child that they are the best at being themselves!

Giving up Old Things

Help your child talk about feelings and learn more about growing.

You'll Need

• Nothing

Things to Talk About

• Did you ever want to keep wearing something that was too small?
• How would you feel if you saw someone else wearing your old clothes?

Directions

1. Tell your child about a time you had to give up a piece of clothing you had grown out of.

2. Talk to your child about why sometimes we have to pass on old things.

Remind your child that it's good to donate things you can't use anymore.

Take Your Time

Help your child practice waiting and develop the ability to keep trying.

You'll Need

• Blocks or boxes
• Sweaters, shirts or other clothing with fasteners
• Paper
• Crayons or markers

Directions

1. Ask your child to think of a time when they had to wait for your attention while you were doing something else, like preparing a meal or fixing something that broke. Talk about how it was important that you took your time to do the job right.

2. Let your child choose an activity—stacking blocks, buttoning clothes or drawing a picture. Ask them to hurry through it once, and then do it again while taking their time.

Sometimes you have to hurry, but you can ask for help if you need it.

Things to Talk About

• What happened when you hurried?
• Was it different when you did it carefully?

Remembering

Help your child develop their memory.

You'll Need

- Paintings, drawings or crafts that were made by your child when they were younger
- Toys that used to be your child's favorite
- Old photos of your child

Directions

1. Show your child their old art projects. Do they remember making them? Do they remember playing with their old toys?

2. Show your child the pictures of themselves. Do they remember what was happening when that picture was taken?

Things to Talk About

- Do you have a favorite memory?
- What is the earliest thing you remember?

Point out the ways your child has grown since these memories.

Cleaning up a Mess

Help your child talk about feelings.

You'll Need

- Nothing

Remind your child that cleaning up after an accident is not a punishment.

Directions

1. Talk to your child about a time you tried to help someone and accidentally spilled or broke something. Make sure to talk about how you felt about it.

2. Can your child think of a time when they did the same thing? What's the best thing to do when this happens?

Things to Talk About

- How can you clean up spilled milk or paint, or get crayon off a wall?

Let's Do It Again

Help your child practice making choices.

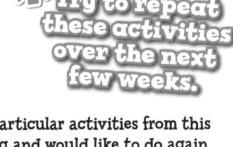

Try to repeat these activities over the next few weeks.

You'll Need

- Pencil or pen
- Paper

Things to Talk About

- Do you have the materials you need to do one of those activities again now?

- What kinds of activities do you like best?

Directions

1. Ask your child if there were any particular activities from this book that they have enjoyed doing and would like to do again one day.

2. Together, make a list of favorite activities they have done. If your child has trouble remembering, ask if they can think of a specific art project, a pretending activity or a dance or music activity.

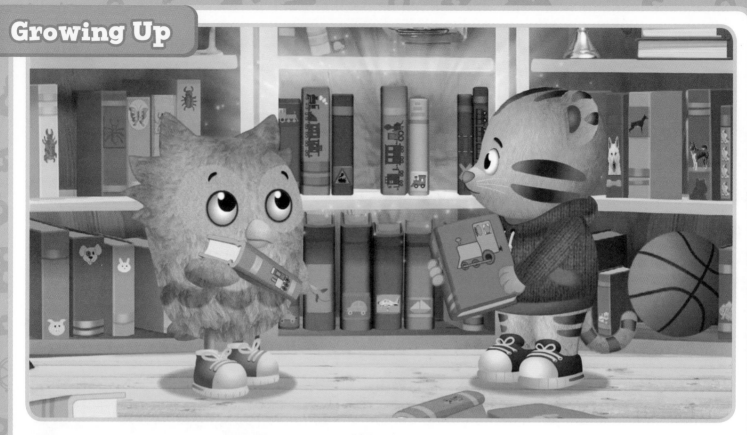

Everything in Its Place

Help your child learn to clean up and develop self-control.

You'll Need

- Your child's toys, books or clothes and bedding
- Containers for sorting them

Directions

1. If your child has a particularly messy toy box or bookshelf, or their clothes or bedding tends to get jumbled together, this is a good activity for teaching organization.

2. Help your child sort their possessions into the different containers. Make picture and word labels for the containers so your child can keep things in their places.

Things to Talk About

- Is it easier to find things when they have a place?
- Does a room look nicer when everything is put away?

Encourage your child to return toys and books to their places before choosing a new one.

It Takes Practice

Help your child develop their memory and the ability to keep trying.

You'll Need

- Words to a poem or song

Things to Talk About

- What is your favorite song?
- Do you want to memorize it?

Directions

1. Choose a short, familiar poem or song to read or sing to your child. Go over the words with them and encourage them to repeat each line after you. See how long it takes for your child to memorize a whole verse.

This is a good activity to do while riding in a car or waiting for their turn.

Keeping Yourself Safe

Help your child talk about feelings and learn about limits.

You'll Need

- Nothing

Directions

1. Start by talking to your child about why people wear helmets when riding a bicycle. Can they think of other things people do to stay safe? Examples include wearing a seatbelt in the car, holding hands while crossing the street, picking up toys so people don't trip, etc.

Things to Talk About

- What does it mean to be safe? Parents need to know where their children are and what they are doing so they can help them stay safe.

Reassure your child that you will help them stay safe.

181

Growing and Changing

Help your child learn more about growing and feel proud of accomplishments.

You'll Need

- Long strips of paper
- Markers

Things to Talk About

- Do you think you'll get even taller?
- What are some new things you want to learn?

Save the list and revisit it (and the mark on the wall) in a few months to see how your child has grown.

Directions

1. Talk to your child about the different ways they're growing on both the outside and the inside. Ask your child if they're taller than they used to be. How do they know?

2. Ask your child to come up with some "inside" ways of growing. This might include:
   - Using the bathroom
   - Dressing themselves
   - Riding a tricycle
   - Using a fork

3. Make a list of all the things your child has learned to do recently and tape a strip of paper on the wall that marks your child's current height.

Everyone is big enough to do something!

183

Feelings & Imagination

Learn to be creative and express feelings in healthy ways.

Remind your child they are the best at being themselves!

Kings and Queens

Help your child have fun trying out different roles.

You'll Need

- Paper crowns
- Fancy hats or scarves
- Plastic or costume jewelry
- Flowing material for capes and robes
- Mirror

Directions

1. Decide on a story to act out with your child. Perhaps there is about to be a royal wedding or the king and queen must make a royal declaration.

2. Help your child dress up like a king or queen. Construct paper crowns, fashion robes out of loose material such as a towel or tablecloth and layer on costume jewelry.

3. Let your child parade around in front of a mirror and act out a royal story.

Things to Talk About

- What do you think kings and queens do?
- Why do they dress this way?
- How do you feel when you're wearing a crown?

Getting Dressed

Help your child develop their imagination.

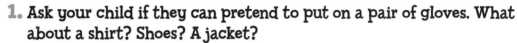 You can also pretend to brush teeth, comb hair and take a bath.

You'll Need

- Nothing

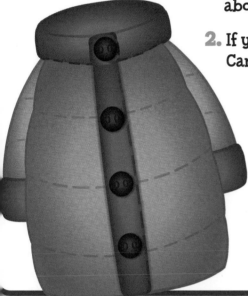

Directions

1. Ask your child if they can pretend to put on a pair of gloves. What about a shirt? Shoes? A jacket?

2. If you like, play a game by pretending to put on a piece of clothing. Can your child guess what that piece of clothing is?

Things to Talk About

- What other things can you pretend to put on?

- Could you pretend to be getting dressed up for a fancy event?

Digging a Hole

Help your child express strong feelings in appropriate ways.

You'll Need

- Old spoons
- Plastic shovels
- Small metal shovel or garden tools
- Plastic containers or pails

Directions

1. If you have a yard (or can go to a park with a sandbox), let your child dig a hole with the tools you've provided.

2. Encourage your child to come up with a pretend reason for digging the hole. They could be looking for treasure or making a home for a pretend animal.

 This activity can also be done in snow.

Things to Talk About

- Digging a hole is something someone could do when they are upset. What are other things you might want to do when you are angry?

Dancing Day

Help your child express their feelings through movement and dance.

You'll Need

- Enough room for dancing

This is a good activity for a group of children.

Things to Talk About

- Do you like to dance?
- How does dancing make you feel?
- Do you like dancing alone or with other people?

Directions

1. Without turning on music, ask your child to move in ways that express how they feel. Ask them to make up a name for their dance.

2. Ask your child to make up a happy dance, sad dance, angry dance and sleepy dance.

3. Turn on some music. Ask your child to dance the way the music feels.

What Can Babies Do?

Help your child learn more about growing and understand the difference between real and pretend.

You'll Need

- Nothing

Things to Talk About

- What can you do now that you couldn't when you were a baby?
- Why don't people stay babies?

Directions

1. Ask your child what things a baby can do. What toys can they use? What sounds can they make? How do they move?

2. Ask your child to show you some toys they played with as a baby. Let them pretend to be a baby again, but remind them when it's time to stop playing.

 Show your child pictures from when they were a baby.

Important Talk

Help your child use play to talk about feelings.

Things to Talk About

- Remind your child that "there's time for you and baby, too."

You'll Need

- Baby doll
- Baby bottle
- Blanket

Directions

1. Set out the baby doll along with the bottle and blanket. Ask your child to pretend the doll is a real baby. How would they care for it?

2. Encourage your child to pretend to give the baby a bath, feed it and rock it to sleep.

 This is a good activity if you or someone you know is expecting a baby.

When a Pet Dies

Help your child talk about feelings and express strong feelings in appropriate ways.

💡 **A favorite toy or blanket might make your child feel more secure during this talk.**

You'll Need

- Paper
- Crayons
- Favorite stuffed toys or blankets

Things to Talk About

- Explain that it's OK to be sad when a pet or someone you love dies.

Directions

1. Talk to your child about how you felt when a pet of yours died. Encourage your child to ask you questions about that experience.

2. If this conversation brings out strong feelings, your child might find it helpful to draw or paint when you're done talking.

The Missing Pieces

Help your child accept individual differences and recognize feelings.

You'll Need

- Puzzle that has missing pieces
- Heavy cardboard
- Markers or crayons
- Scissors

Directions

1. Set out the puzzle with a missing piece and help your child put it together. How do they feel when they can't finish because a piece is missing?

2. Help your child make a new puzzle piece from the cardboard. Let your child color it to resemble the missing piece.

Things to Talk About

- Can you think of a time when something was missing that you needed? How did you feel?

Put the puzzle together over the cardboard and trace any missing pieces.

Scary Sounds

Help your child express feelings of fear through play.

You'll Need

- Pie tins, metal bowls or cake pans
- Wooden spoons

Directions

1. Ask your child if there are any sounds they think are scary. Can they name the things that make those sounds?

2. Ask your child to bang the spoons on the pans to make loud noises. Can they also make soft "scary" sounds? What about with their voices?

Things to Talk About

- Is a sound less scary when you know where it's coming from?
- What kind of sounds can you make that aren't scary?

I Feel Jealous When...

Help your child recognize and talk about jealousy and express it in appropriate ways.

You'll Need

- Paper
- Markers or crayons

Directions

1. Tell your child about a time when you felt jealous, then ask your child if they have ever felt that way. For example, when a younger sibling was born, when a friend got a toy they wanted or when an older sibling got to do something they weren't allowed to.

2. Together, think of some healthy ways for your child to express their jealousy. They can take a deep breath, tell someone how they feel, paint or draw a picture, or remind themself of the ways they are special too.

Things to Talk About

- Do you think everybody has felt jealous before?

Remind your child of Daniel Tiger's song, "When you feel jealous talk about it, and we'll figure something out."

The Clown in Me

Help your child talk about attention and learn to use words.

Telling someone how you feel is a better way to explain what you need.

You'll Need

- Silly hat or wig
- Clown costume (optional)

Directions

1. Ask your child if they ever feel like acting silly. Can they tell you why? (e.g. They feel like it, they want to make someone laugh, they want attention, etc.)

2. Let your child act like a clown just for fun, by making faces, walking in a funny way and wearing the wig and a costume if you have one.

Things to Talk About

- Do you like the attention you get when you act silly?
- Can you ask someone to play with you when you want attention?

Talking About Accidents

Help your child learn more about feelings.

You'll Need

- Nothing

Directions

1. Tell your child about a time when you accidentally ruined or broke something. Make sure to talk about how doing that made you feel. If you were afraid to tell people what you did, tell your child about that too.

End this activity by talking about good things you have done too.

Things to Talk About

- Have you ever done something bad and then hid it? How did that feel?

193

Talking About Limits

Help your child learn about limits.

You'll Need

- Nothing

Directions

1. Ask your child if they can name some of the limits or rules you have at home. This might include rules about:
   - Sharing
   - Using scissors and other tools
   - Crossing streets
   - What things they can eat
   - When they have to go to bed

Talk about how adults and children sometimes have different limits.

Things to Talk About

- Why do we have these rules?
- Are there other rules you think everyone should follow?

Angry Feelings

Help your child talk about anger and express it in appropriate ways.

You'll Need

- Paper
- Pencil, pen or marker

Directions

1. Tell your child about a time when you were upset and said or did something that hurt someone. How did you feel afterward? How do you think the other person felt?

2. Make a list of things you can do when you're upset that don't hurt anybody. Remember, "When you feel so mad that you want to roar, take a deep breath and count to four."

Things to Talk About

- Can you think of a time when you were angry? What did you do?

Remind your child that everyone gets angry sometimes.

I Used to Be Afraid

Pair this activity with Flying Ghosts (page 25).

Help your child recognize and talk about fear.

You'll Need

- Nothing

Directions

1. Tell your child about something that used to frighten you when you were their age. Tell your child how you worked on your fear.

Things to Talk About

- Is there anything you used to be afraid of?
- Why aren't you afraid anymore?

Time to Myself

Help your child learn more about privacy.

Remind your child you can want alone time and still love the people around you.

You'll Need

• Nothing

Directions

1. Talk to your child about a time when you weren't feeling well and acted a little irritable toward them. Point out that grown-ups need rest or time to themselves, just like children do. Like Teacher Harriet says, "Sometimes you want to be alone. You can find a place of your very own."

2. Come up with a list of things your child might like to do when they want to be left alone, like taking a nap, looking at books or watching a video.

Things to Talk About

• Can you think of a time when you wanted to be left alone?

• What is your favorite thing to do by yourself?

Making a Map

Help your child get comfortable with your absence.

You'll Need

- Large sheet of paper
- Markers or crayons
- Toy cars or people

Directions

1. Your child may feel better when you go to work or run an errand if they know where you are. Make a simple map showing where your house is, where your work is, where the grocery store is, etc.

2. Lay the map on a table and let your child use the toys to trace trips from home to work, work to the store and so on.

Things to Talk About

- Why do parents need to go to work?
- What ways do you show that you missed your parents while they were gone?

💡 **Remind your child that grown-ups come back.**

What Is Love?

Help your child understand the concept of love and how to express it.

You'll Need

- Paper
- Pencil, pen or marker

💡 **Sing "Find Your Own Way To Say I Love You" (page 281).**

Directions

1. Ask your child what they think love is. Make a list of their answers.

2. Ask your child if they have ever been angry with someone they love. When they were finished being angry, did they still love them?

Things to Talk About

- What are some of the ways you show people you love them?
- Does everybody show their love the same way?

Your child might like to draw a picture of a fun time they had with their friend.

Saying Goodbye

Help your child work on feelings about separation.

You'll Need

• Nothing

Directions

1. Has your child ever had a friend who moved away or who they used to see at preschool or the playground and no longer do? Ask your child what they remember best about that person. How did they feel when their friend had to leave?

2. If you can still get in contact with this person, your child might like to send them a letter or call them on the phone.

Things to Talk About

• Are there any special things you could do to say goodbye to someone?

Talking About Sharing

Help your child practice sharing and learn more about privacy.

You'll Need

- Nothing

Directions

1. Ask your child how they feel when they have to share their toys. Talk about how sharing means taking turns. It doesn't mean you have to give up a toy right away; you can finish playing with it first.

Things to Talk About

- Which toys are your favorite?
- Is there anything you don't have to share? (Special toys, blankets, etc.)

Remind your child they can always decide if they want to share their thoughts and feelings.

When Something Breaks

Help your child recover from disappointment and try again.

You'll Need

- Building blocks or small cardboard boxes

Directions

1. Ask your child to work with you to use the blocks or boxes to build a tower or castle.

2. While you're building, talk to your child about a time when you broke something. Tell them how you felt about it.

Things to Talk About

- Have you ever broken something?
- What if someone accidentally knocked down our tower?
- Could it be built again?

199

Why Do People Cry?

Help your child talk about crying and what it means.

You'll Need

- Nothing

Sometimes people cry when they are happy too.

Directions

1. Talk to your child about crying. Have they ever seen a friend crying or someone crying on *Daniel Tiger*? How do they think that person felt?

2. Name some of the feelings people show when they are crying. This could include:
- Sadness
- Loneliness
- Anger
- Fear
- Pain

Things to Talk About

- Can you talk about something that made you feel like crying?
- Did you feel better after you cried?

All About Families

Help your child learn more about their world and the nature of families.

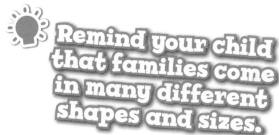

You'll Need

- Paper
- Markers or crayons
- Pictures of family members (optional)

Directions

1. Ask your child to draw a picture of each person in their family and see if they can name them all. (Or see if they can name family members in photos.)

2. See if your child can tell you how each family member is related (e.g. their aunt's daughter is their cousin).

Things to Talk About

- Who are the people in your family?
- Do families always live in the same house?

Remind your child that families come in many different shapes and sizes.

Pantomime Feelings

Help your child learn different ways people communicate and learn more about their bodies.

You'll Need

- Paper
- Hand mirror
- Markers or crayons

Things to Talk About

- Does everybody look the same way when they're sad?
- Can you always tell how someone is feeling just by looking at them?

Directions

1. Ask your child to name different feelings, like happy, sad and angry.

2. Pantomime different feelings and see if your child can guess which one you are showing them.

3. Let your child use the hand mirror to practice pantomiming feelings too. How would they look if they were surprised? Afraid? Happy?

Misunderstandings

Help your child learn to listen carefully.

You'll Need

• Nothing

If your child isn't sure what you said, ask them to guess.

Directions

1. Tell your child about a time when a person said something to you and you thought that person meant something else. How did you feel when you found out what that person really meant? (Disappointed? Sad? Glad?)

2. Play a game where you whisper a silly nonsense phrase in your child's ear and see if they can repeat what you said out loud. If your child is older and you are doing this activity with a group, have them whisper the phrase around in a game of "Telephone."

Things to Talk About

• Was the phrase the same at the end of the game?

• Did you have to listen closely to understand what was being whispered?

Pretending

Help your child understand the difference between real and pretend.

You'll Need

- Nothing

Things to Talk About

- Do you like to pretend to be something you're not?
- How can you tell if something is real or pretend?

Directions

1. Talk about how sometimes people get confused between real and pretend. Can your child think of a time when they weren't sure if something was real? They might think of:
   - Someone dressed up at Halloween
   - Another child pretending to be a monster or animal
   - A puppet on a hand
   - A clown at a circus
   - A scary dream

Pretend to be something silly, like an elephant or an airplane.

Disappointments

Help your child understand that wishing can't make things happen.

You'll Need

- Paper
- Crayons or markers

Directions

1. Ask your child to think of a time when they hoped something would happen and then felt disappointed when it didn't.

2. Ask your child to tell you how they felt. What were they disappointed about? Did they feel angry? Sad? What helped them feel better?

3. If they want, have your child draw a picture of something they've imagined themselves doing, like flying or doing magic.

Things to Talk About

- What are some pretend things that could never actually happen (e.g. a dog driving a car, a horse being able to talk)?

It can be fun to pretend as long as we remember pretending isn't what makes things happen.

Help Me, Don't Help Me

Help your child learn to do things independently and recognize feelings.

You'll Need

- Nothing

Remind your child that everyone needs help sometimes, even grown-ups.

Directions

1. Ask your child to name some things they can do all on their own. This might include:
- Putting on shoes
- Zipping a jacket
- Washing their face
- Brushing their teeth
- Putting away toys

2. Ask your child to name some things they still need help to do, like taking a bath or using a knife.

Things to Talk About

- Are you proud of the things you know how to do?
- How do you feel when you need help to do something?

Can Wishes Come True?

Help your child understand that wishing can't make things happen.

You'll Need

- Nothing

Directions

1. Can your child think of something they wished for? Did it come true? If it did come true, what made it happen?

2. Ask your child if they have any wishes right now. Is there anything they could do to make it happen?

Things to Talk About

- Have you ever wished for something bad or sad to happen? Most people do, but wishes can't make those things happen either.

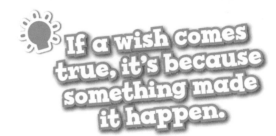 If a wish comes true, it's because something made it happen.

A Place of My Own

Help your child learn more about privacy.

You'll Need

- Blanket or sheet
- Two chairs or a small table
- Pillows, books, etc. (optional)

Directions

1. Have your child help you make a small fort by draping a blanket over two chairs or a small table. Make the fort more cozy by adding pillows, soft toys and favorite books.

2. Remind your child that "Sometimes you want to be alone. You can find a place of your very own." Ask your child if there are any times when they feel like being alone.

3. Encourage your child to spend some quiet time alone in the fort.

Things to Talk About

- What other places can you go when you want to be alone?
- Why is it important to let other people have alone time when they ask for it?

Saying What You Feel

Help your child use play to talk about feelings.

You'll Need

- Nothing

Directions

1. Tell your child about a time when you wanted to tell someone you liked them but you felt too shy to do so. Can your child think of a time when they felt that way too?

2. See if your child can come up with different ways to show people how they feel. This might include:

- Giving a smile
- Drawing a picture
- Making a present
- Making up a song
- Preparing a meal

You might want to sing "Find Your Own Way To Say I Love You" (page 281).

Things to Talk About

- Can you think of some ways to overcome shyness?

- Could you practice telling someone how you feel?

An Imaginary Land

Help your child develop their imagination.

You'll Need

- Key made out of cardboard

Directions

1. Give your child the cardboard key and ask them to pretend it opens the door to an imaginary land.

2. Ask your child to "use" the key. Can they tell you about the land they've imagined?

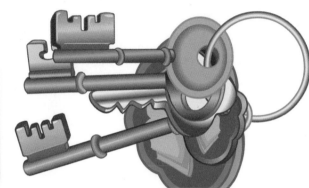

Multiple children can take turns describing imaginary lands.

Things to Talk About

- What do you see when you open the door?
- Who do you meet?
- What could happen in this land?

Going Away, Coming Back

Help your child work on feelings about separation.

You'll Need

- Bell or whistle

Directions

1. Tell your child about a time when you had mixed feelings about coming home, perhaps when you were spending time with friends or coming home from a vacation.

2. Play a game about going away and coming back. When you give the signal, your child should go hide (but stay within earshot; it's a good idea to set up boundaries for this game). Let your child know that even though they're having fun hiding, they must come back as quick as they can when you signal again.

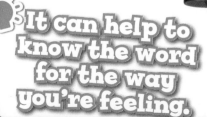

It can help to know the word for the way you're feeling.

Things to Talk About

- Have you ever had mixed feelings about coming home?
- Do you know what the word "ambivalent" means?

Unhappy Feelings

Help your child talk about feelings and express them through art.

You'll Need

- Mirror
- Crayons
- Paper

Directions

1. Can your child think of a time when they were unhappy about something? What are some ways they can let people know they are unhappy? They could say they feel unhappy, cry, go off to bed alone or look sad.

2. Can your child show you how they look when they are unhappy? Let them see their face in the mirror when they do this.

3. Have your child draw a picture of the way they feel when they are unhappy.

Things to Talk About

- What can you do to feel better when you are unhappy?
- Do you have a favorite toy that makes you feel better?

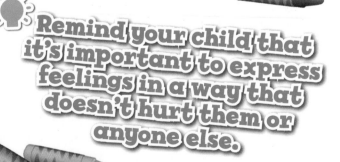

Remind your child that it's important to express feelings in a way that doesn't hurt them or anyone else.

Playing as Witches

Help your child understand the difference between real and pretend.

You'll Need

- Witch's hat
- Black cape or piece of dark material
- Dress-up skirt
- Magic wand (toy or made from cardboard)
- Mirror

Save the costume for future pretend playtimes.

Directions

1. Encourage your child to dress up like a witch. How does a witch talk? Can you laugh like a witch or make your face look like an angry witch?

2. If they want to, help your child come up with a story about a witch. Can they act it out?

Things to Talk About

- Are you a real witch or a pretend one?
- Are there any real witches?

Pretending About the Future

Help your child develop their imagination and learn more about growing.

You'll Need

- Ball
- Scarf
- Dress-up clothes and accessories (optional)

Things to Talk About

- Do crystal balls really work?
- Can anyone predict the future?

Directions

1. Cover any large ball with a scarf to turn it into a "magic" crystal ball. Ask your child to tell you what they "see" in the ball.

2. Ask more questions, like:
    - "What do you see yourself doing when you grow up?"
    - "Will you have your own children to take care of?"
    - "What does your home look like?"

Take Something Along

Help your child use play to talk about feelings.

You'll Need

- Nothing

Directions

1. Ask your child if they have ever felt nervous before a new experience, like going to the doctor or riding a bus or airplane for the first time. Did they take any special belongings or toys along to help them feel more comfortable?

2. Encourage your child to pretend they are going to school for the first time. What could they take along with them to make them feel better?

Let your child know when they are scared, they don't have to share these important toys with anyone else.

Things to Talk About

- Are new things always scary?

- Are you ever excited to do something new?

210

Super Capes

Help your child understand the difference between real and pretend.

You'll Need

- Soft, light blanket
- Safety pins

Things to Talk About

- What kind of "superpowers" would you like to have?
- Can you ever really have these powers or just pretend to have them?

Directions

1. Help your child put on a "cape" by pinning a blanket around their shoulders and encourage them to pretend they are a superhero. Remind your child that they cannot knock things over or throw toys.

2. Have your child pretend to do something heroic, like saving a town or stopping a monster.

Do this activity outside so your child can run.

Windstorm

Help your child express feelings through movement and dance.

You'll Need

- Scarves, capes or soft fabric
- Crayons or markers
- Paper

Directions

1. Let your child pretend to be a windstorm by flapping around with scarves, capes or pieces of soft material. Encourage your child to make blowing sounds as they move. Can they show you the difference between a soft breeze and a gusty wind?

2. When you're ready to end the activity, help your child calm down by asking them to pretend to be leaves that flutter in a gentle breeze.

3. Let your child use the crayons and paper to make a picture of a windstorm.

Things to Talk About

- How do you feel on a very windy day?
- Are you safe inside your home?

An Airplane Ride

Help your child learn more about their world and develop their imagination.

You'll Need

- Large cardboard box
- Markers
- Tote bag or small suitcase

You might want to give your child a small snack while they're in the airplane.

Directions

1. Has your child ever been on an airplane? Do they remember what it was like? If not, encourage them to tell you what they think it would be like.

2. Construct or draw wings on the sides of the box and let your child sit inside with their "luggage."

Things to Talk About

- Where is the plane "flying" to?
- What will it be like there?

Let's Imagine

Help your child develop creative play and their imagination.

You'll Need
- Nothing

Directions

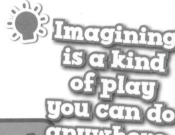

1. Can your child think of a time when they can't move around and play as they'd like, such as when they're buckled up in the car? Come up with a few different ways they can use their imagination during those times. For example:
   - Imagine they are on a rocket ship
     - Play "I Spy"
     - Take turns telling familiar stories

Imagining is a kind of play you can do anywhere.

Things to Talk About
- Can you use your imagination to play when you have to be quiet?

Going for a Ride

Help your child develop their imagination.

You'll Need
- Chairs
- Belts
- Dress-up clothes and accessories

Directions

1. Help your child set up the chairs as though they were seats in a car. Put a belt on each chair as a pretend seatbelt.

2. Encourage your child to sit on their chair and remind them to fasten their seatbelt. Ask your child where they want to pretend they are going on this ride.

Things to Talk About
- Can you imagine you are driving on a safari?
- What animals do you "see"?

If you are doing this with multiple children, have them take turns going for rides.

Dreaming

Help your child talk about feelings.

💡 Remind your child that dreams may seem real but they are only thoughts in pictures.

You'll Need

- Paper (optional)
- Crayons or markers (optional)

Things to Talk About

- What did you daydream about?
- Was it something that could really happen?

Directions

1. Ask your child if they can remember the last dream they had. Was it scary? Silly? Weird?

2. Ask your child if they have ever heard of daydreaming. Explain that daydreaming is a time when people think about things that could be or what they want to do.

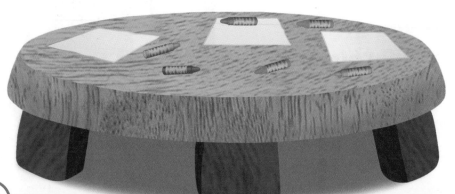

3. Encourage your child to daydream about things that might happen or places they would like to go. Then, if they'd like, they can draw a picture of their daydream.

Shadow Play

Help your child develop their imagination and use play to work on feelings.

You'll Need

- Bright light (like a desk lamp or flashlight)

Remind your child that they can always talk to you about the things that frighten them.

Directions

1. Tell your child about a time when you saw something that turned out to be very different from what you thought it was. Was it a funny or scary experience?

2. Shine a bright light on the wall and encourage your child to use their fingers to make shadow puppets. Do the shadows look like anything else?

Things to Talk About

- Are the shadows scary when you know what they are?
- Have you ever thought something was very different from what it was?

There's Work to Do

Help your child learn more about work and develop creative play.

You'll Need

- Blocks, cars, trucks, dolls or action figures
- Modeling dough, plastic dishes, plastic utensils
- Books, paper, pencils, markers

Things to Talk About

- Do you think that job will be fun?
- Are there more jobs you would like to try?

Directions

1. Ask your child if they know what they want to be when they grow up. Encourage your child to pretend to do that job with the materials you've gathered. For example:
   - Builders, construction workers, repair people
   - Nurses, doctors, dentists
   - Bakers, cooks, restaurant owners
   - Teachers, librarians, authors

Let your child know they can pretend to do a different job another day.

I Wonder

Help your child develop their curiosity and feel comfortable asking about things.

Remind your child that when you wonder, you can try to find out more.

You'll Need

- Paper
- Marker

Directions

1. Help your child make a list of things they wonder about. For example:
- I wonder how balls are made.
- I wonder what happens to snow when it melts.
- I wonder where milk comes from.

2. Encourage your child to come up with their own explanation for each thing they wonder about.

MILK

Things to Talk About

- How would you find out the answer to this?
- Is there anyone you can ask?

Yes and No

Help your child develop self-control and learn to express strong feelings in appropriate ways.

You'll Need

- Nothing

Directions

1. Ask your child how they feel when they're told no. What are some of the things they know they can't do? (Throwing balls in the house, hitting others, going in the street, etc.)

2. Help your child think of things they can do, like throwing balls in the yard, using words to say they're angry or playing at a playground.

Things to Talk About

- What are some things you can do when you're upset or feeling angry?
- Can you draw a picture or tell someone how you feel?

The Truth Will Make Me Free

Help your child recognize and talk about feelings.

You'll Need

- Nothing

Things to Talk About

- Did you ever think it would be scary to tell the truth but it felt good when you finally did it?

Directions

1. Ask your child to think of a time when they were afraid to tell someone the truth. It might help to ask if they:
   - Felt afraid about a trip or visit to someone
   - Didn't want to give a kiss to somebody
   - Made a mess and felt afraid someone would be angry
   - Were afraid of the dark but didn't want to say so

Remind your child that there's nothing wrong with feeling scared, but telling the truth will make them feel better.

217

Saying I Am Sorry

Help your child talk about feelings.

You'll Need

💡 You might suggest talking about the mistake, writing a note or hugging the person.

- Nothing

Directions

1. Talk with your child about a time they made a mistake that hurt someone's feelings. If your child has a hard time "telling on themselves," start by talking about a time where you did the same thing. You could also ask your child about how they feel when someone else makes a mistake and it hurts their feelings.

Things to Talk About

- What does it mean to feel sorry?

- Remind your child: "Saying sorry is the first step. Then, how can I help?"

Puppet Play

Help your child use play to work on feelings.

You'll Need

- Hand puppets or sock puppets (see page 39)

Directions

1. If you are making the puppets yourself, this could be a good chance to ask your child how they feel when they make a mistake on a project.

2. Encourage your child to act out a story they've made up by using the puppets. You could start by having one puppet talk to the other about a mistake they've made.

Things to Talk About

- What can you do when you make a mistake?

- What did you learn from it?

Ask your child the puppets' names, then make sure to use them to encourage pretending.

Thank-You Messages

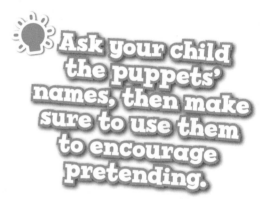

Help your child learn different ways people communicate and recognize and use symbols.

You'll Need

- Paper

- Pencils, markers or crayons

- Envelopes

Directions

1. Talk to your child about the importance of saying thank you when someone does something for them.

2. Ask your child to think of someone who has done something special for them lately. Help them make a thank-you note for this person.

Things to Talk About

- Do you know what a message is?

- What are some other ways people send messages?

You may want to sing "Thank You For Everything You Do."

A Pretend Dentist

Help your child try out different roles.

You'll Need

- Toothbrushes
- Dental floss
- Tongue depressor or ice pop stick
- Dolls

Directions

1. If your child has been to the dentist, start by asking them what they remember about their visit.

2. Ask your child if they want to pretend to be a dentist. They can use dolls as patients and use the ice pop stick as a dental instrument.

Things to Talk About

- What kinds of things does the dentist say to you?
- How does the dentist help you?

Puppets can also make for good pretend patients.

Telephone Talk

Help your child work on feelings about separation.

You'll Need

- 1 or 2 toy phones

Directions

1. Talk to your child about where you or another adult works and what you do while you're there. Ask your child if they're ever upset that they can't talk to you or someone else because they're at work.

2. Suggest to your child that they have a pretend phone conversation with the person they're missing.

 If you don't have a toy phone, make a pretend one out of a block or small box.

Things to Talk About

- Why do people have to go to work?
- What other things can you do when you miss them?

An Imaginary Book

Help your child develop their imagination and creativity.

Your child might like to turn the imaginary book into a real one by filling in words and pictures.

You'll Need

- Paper
- Stapler
- Markers or pens
- Construction paper

Directions

1. Assemble a blank booklet by stapling together five or six pieces of paper. Use construction paper to make a cover for the booket. Add a title to the cover, like "*An Imaginary Book* by [child's name]."

2. Show your child the book and encourage them to make up their own story to fill it. Let your child sit in your lap and slowly turn the pages as they tell their story.

Things to Talk About

- How would you illustrate your imaginary book?
- Does the story change every time?

Learning to Pretend

Help your child develop imagination and express feelings through movement and dance.

You'll Need

- Music
- Scarves

Directions

1. Ask your child to think of something silly to be, like the wind or an elephant. Encourage them to use the scarves to help in their pretending (e.g. use the scarf as an elephant's trunk).

2. Play music and let your child move around to it while pretending to be whatever they choose.

Things to Talk About

- What else could you pretend to be?

- What kind of music do you think we should play for this?

This is a good activity for a group.

Up in the Air

Help your child develop their imagination.

You'll Need

• Nothing

Things to Talk About

• What do you think it would be like to be a bird? Or ride in a spaceship?

Directions

1. Take your child for a walk and pause to look up every once in a while. What do they see? (Birds, planes, clouds, tree branches, etc.)

2. When you get back home, ask your child to think about the things they saw up in the sky. Can they imagine what it would be like to be up there, looking down below?

 Make up a story about being a bird.

When you pretend, you can be anything!

Playing Together

Practice kindness, cooperation and working out problems with one another.

Taking Turns

Help your child practice sharing, taking turns and waiting.

You'll Need

- Tricycle or other riding toy

Directions

1. Using a tricycle or other toy, help the children practice taking turns. Have the children help decide the order everyone will go in and how to decide when each turn is over.

Things to Talk About

- Ask the children what "taking turns" means.

- Why do we sometimes have to take turns?

 Remind your child that "you can take a turn, then I'll get it back!"

Playing Ball Games

Help your child develop coordination.

You'll Need

- Several balls
- Laundry basket

Directions

1. Talk about where and how you play with a ball. Tell your child we don't hit people with balls, keep them in the yard and never go in the street to get a ball.

2. Set out an empty laundry basket. Give your child a ball and ask your child to try to toss the ball into the basket.

3. If your child is having an easy time, move the basket farther away.

Things to Talk About

- Is it easier to toss the ball in the basket if you are looking at the basket?
- What happens if you let go of the ball at different times?

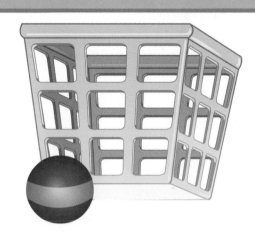

Flying Discs

Help your child develop creative play.

Cut a thin "pie slice" from the disc to help it fly better.

You'll Need

- Cardboard
- Scissors
- Crayons or markers (optional)

Directions

1. Cut a 5- to 6-inch circle from a piece of cardboard and let the children color it in. It might be good to divide it into sections so each child can color their own part.

2. Go outside and encourage the children to play with their new disc. They can take turns tossing it and making it spin or practice tossing it to one another.

Things to Talk About

- Can everyone play with the disc at once?
- How can you make it fair?

Working Together

Help your child practice working together cooperatively.

If your child wants to do something by themself right now, that's OK too.

You'll Need

- Toy that requires 2 people (swing, ball, seesaw)
- Paper
- Markers, crayons or nontoxic paint and brushes

Directions

1. Encourage the children to work together on a project or play a game that requires a friend. This might mean taking turns pushing one another on the swings, using a seesaw or rolling or tossing a ball back and forth. For an inside activity, children could work together on a drawing or painting.

Things to Talk About

- Is it fun to do things together?
- Do you know what "cooperation" means?

A Block Tower

Help your child develop coordination, practice taking turns and recognize feelings.

You'll Need

- Set of small blocks or boxes

Directions

1. Spread out the blocks on the floor. Make sure you set up in an area where the falling tower won't knock anything else over.

2. Place one block in the center. Have each child take turns adding blocks to the tower.

3. Continue taking turns until the tower falls over.

Things to Talk About

- What feelings did you have while waiting for the tower to fall over?

- Why do you think the tower fell over?

Shoebox Harp

Help your child develop creative play and recognize likeness and difference.

You'll Need

- One shoebox for each child

- Different-sized rubber bands (3 or 4 for each child)

Things to Talk About

- Do different boxes make different sounds?

- Do thick and thin rubber bands make different sounds?

Let the children form their own "band" and try to play their harps together.

Directions

1. Give each child a shoebox without its lid and a few rubber bands of different thicknesses.

2. Help the children stretch the rubber bands around the boxes and show them how to pluck or strum the rubber bands. Listen together for different sounds.

Guess What I Am

Help your child try out different roles and develop their imagination.

You'll Need

- Nothing

Act like a chef, bus driver or doctor.

Directions

1. Start the game by letting the children know you're going to be acting out a certain occupation. Then, pantomime movements and see if the children can guess what you are pretending to be.

2. Once the children have guessed what you are pretending to be, they might like to take turns pretending to do a certain job, too.

Things to Talk About

- Do you know what you want to be when you grow up?

- What kinds of things are you interested in?

Guess Which Hand

Help your child practice taking turns.

You'll Need

- Button or other small object

Making up a story is also something you can do anywhere.

Directions

1. Can the children tell you about a time when they were disappointed because they couldn't go somewhere or do something they planned?

2. Tell the children that "Guess Which Hand" is a game they can play anywhere, as long as they have someone to play with. One child hides the button in one of their hands, then the other guesses which hand it's in. When a child guesses correctly, they get to hide the button next.

Things to Talk About

- What other things can you do when you feel disappointed?

Paper Mustache

Help your child develop creative play.

You'll Need

- Construction paper
- Safety scissors
- Crayons or markers
- Tape
- Mirror

Things to Talk About

- Does everybody's mustache look the same?
- Does putting on a pretend mustache change who you are on the inside?

You can make beards too.

Directions

1. Ask the children to draw mustaches on the construction paper, color them in and then cut them out.

2. Roll small pieces of tape (or use double-sided tape) and help the children put the mustaches on their faces. Let them see themselves in a mirror to see how different they look.

You can also use a glass to trace the circles.

Traffic Light Game

Help your child develop self-control.

You'll Need

- Construction paper (red, yellow and green)
- Cardboard circle, about 3 inches
- 2 sheets of white printer paper cut in half longways
- Black marker
- Safety scissors
- 3 rulers or sticks (optional)
- Music

Things to Talk About

- Is it hard to move around and pay attention to the lights?
- Is it hard to slow down when you're having fun?

Directions

1. For this game, you'll need three traffic lights. Let the children take turns tracing the cardboard circle to make one circle on each piece of colored paper and three circles each on the white printer paper (like a traffic light).

2. Cut out the colored circles and glue one to each of the lights—a green circle in the bottom on one, a yellow circle in the middle on another and a red circle on top for the third. If you have rulers or ice pop sticks, tape them to the lights to make handles.

3. Play a game by having the children move around as long as you are showing the green light. When you change to yellow, they should begin to slow down. When you show the red light, they must "freeze."

Parachutes

Help your child use their imagination and practice taking turns.

You'll Need

- Handkerchief or square piece of cloth
- String (4 [8-inch] pieces for each parachute)
- Small paper cups or metal nut/washer
- Pencil

Directions

1. Make a simple parachute by tying an 8-inch piece of string to each corner of a handkerchief or piece of cloth. Using a pencil, poke four holes around the rim of a paper cup and fasten the end of each string to the holes. The children can put a small toy in the cup to add the necessary weight to make it float. The ends of the string can also be tied to a nut or washer.

2. Let the children take turns tossing the parachute in the air and watching it open and float to the ground.

Things to Talk About

- Why is it important to take turns?
- What do you think it would be like to be in a real parachute?

Jumping Over the Moon

Help your child develop coordination and the ability to keep trying.

You'll Need

- Crescent-shaped moons (cut from a 10-inch paper circle)
- Tape

You may like to read "Hey Diddle Diddle" after this activity.

Directions

1. How high and how far can the children jump? See if they would like to show you. Tape a crescent moon on the floor and let the children take turns jumping over it. If one moon is easy, see if they can jump over three or four (one at a time) without stopping. Space the moons so there is room to land between each one.

Things to Talk About

- What do you think it's like in space?
- Would you ever want to be in a rocket ship?

I'm Thinking of a Child

Help your child understand and accept individual differences.

You'll Need

- Nothing

Directions

1. Think of one child from the group and give clues by describing something about that child. For example, their hair color, age, likes or dislikes, etc.

2. Keep adding clues until the other children can guess who you are talking about. Then let the children take turns being the one who gives clues.

Things to Talk About

- Do some of the clues apply to more than one person?

- Can you think of a special clue for each child?

Remember that some children may be sensitive about physical differences.

Hide-and-Seek
Help your child practice taking turns.

You'll Need

- Nothing

Directions

1. Start by setting boundaries for hiding so all the children know which areas are off-limits. If the children are younger, keep the game within one or two rooms.

2. Let one or two children be the seekers while the rest of the children hide. Once all the children are found, new seekers can be chosen.

Things to Talk About

- Do you like being the hider or the seeker?

- Does everybody get to be the seeker at some point?

Keep the emphasis on how fun it is to find people, not who remains hidden the longest.

Animal Parade

Help your child develop both their imagination and creative play.

You'll Need

- Upbeat music for marching
- Metal cake or pie pans
- Wooden spoons

Things to Talk About

- Have you ever been to a parade?
- Were there any animals marching in it?

Directions

1. Announce that you are putting on an animal parade. Let each child decide what kind of animal they would like to be. It's OK if some children are the same animal.

2. Decide together where the parade will go and how it will know when to stop.

3. Play the music and let the children walk along the agreed route while making noise with the spoons and pans.

Some children might like to be spectators of the parade.

Tag Stories

Help your child learn to listen carefully and expand their imagination.

You'll Need

• Nothing

Directions

1. Explain to the children that you'll be telling a story all together. One person starts with a sentence or two, then tags another person to tell the next part of the story.

2. It can be helpful to start the story by suggesting what it will be about, such as a child and their pet, three magic wishes or monsters.

If the children are very young, make up the story yourself and let them fill in key words.

Things to Talk About

• Is it fun to make up stories?

• Would the story have been the same with a different group of people telling it?

Winning and Losing

Help your child practice making choices.

💡 Remind the children that they can do the "losing" choice another time.

You'll Need

- Nothing

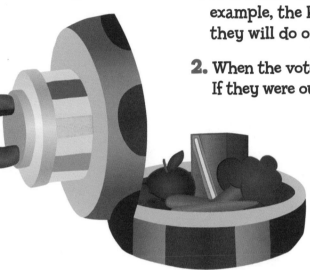

Directions

1. Pick a time to have the children take a vote on something. For example, the kind of juice they have with a snack, what activity they will do or where they want to play.

2. When the vote is over, talk to the children about winning and losing. If they were outvoted, how do they feel?

Things to Talk About

- Is it always important whether you win or lose?
- Can you still have fun with the winning option?

Planning a Party

Help your child practice working cooperatively.

You'll Need

- Paper and pencil
- Scrap materials
- Scissors
- Glue, tape or string

Things to Talk About

- What would the party have been like if you didn't plan for it?

Directions

1. After talking to the other children's parents, plan a "party" for a future playdate (or plan to have one later in the day). Talk to the children about choosing a date and time, making invitations, deciding on a menu, making decorations, etc.

2. Encourage each child to choose something special to do for the party. They can help serve food, decorate, take coats, etc.

A Puppet Show

Help your child develop creative play.

You'll Need

- Large cardboard box
- Markers
- Paint and brushes (optional)
- Puppets, dolls and other toys for props

Directions

1. Make a pretend auditorium by cutting one side out of a cardboard box and another hole for a stage on the opposite side. The children might like to paint or draw curtains on the pretend stage.

2. Using puppets, toys or other props, the children can take turns putting on puppet shows.

Things to Talk About

- What is your favorite story?
- Can you act out a scene you remember?

The children could also sing songs or make up their own stories.

A Pretend Orchestra

Help your child try out different roles and learn to follow directions.

You'll Need

- A recording of instrumental music
- Ruler, wooden spoon or another pretend baton

Directions

1. See if the children can pantomime playing different instruments: violins, harps, trumpets, etc.

2. Make a pretend orchestra with you as the conductor and the children as the musicians. When you give the signal with your "baton," press play on the music and have the children pretend to play. When you give the signal to stop, press pause and have the children put down their "instruments."

Things to Talk About

- Is is hard to pretend and pay attention to the baton?
- Can you hear the different sounds each instrument makes?

I Am Thinking Of...

Help your child learn to use words and practice taking turns.

You'll Need

- Nothing

Directions

1. Start the game by thinking of something specific and then telling the children what sort of thing it is—a fruit, vegetable, animal, color, etc. Everybody gets one guess. If no one guesses right, the thinker gives a clue and everybody takes another guess.

2. Once someone guesses correctly, the other person takes a turn being the thinker and the game continues.

Things to Talk About

- What kinds of clues can you give that are helpful?
- Did you have fun, even if you didn't guess correctly?

Playing with Ramps

Help your child learn more about their world.

You'll Need

- Pieces of heavy cardboard
- Blocks or empty boxes
- Toy cars
- Toy people
- Doll furniture

Directions

1. Using the blocks, cardboard and toy cars, show the children how a ramp makes it easy for the cars to drive up onto higher blocks.

2. How would they think to use ramps to move doll furniture? Can they think of other ways to use ramps while playing with blocks?

Let the children take turns using cars on the ramp.

Things to Talk About

- Can you think of other ways people use ramps in real life? (e.g. for people in wheelchairs or strollers, etc.)

Some Things Belong to Everyone

Help your child practice sharing.

You'll Need

- Paper
- Paint, crayons or markers

Directions

1. Can the children think of some things at a school or library that have to be shared with everyone (e.g. books, furniture, librarians, etc.)? What about at home or on a playground?

2. Set out the paint, crayons or markers and talk about how you will have to share the supplies to make a picture—but each picture belongs to the child who made it.

Remind the children there are some things they don't have to share.

Things to Talk About

- Does it feel good to share?
- Can you take turns using the things you need?

Let's Dance

Help your child express feelings through movement and dance.

You'll Need

- Music
- Scarves

Directions

1. Show the children a video of someone dancing. Can they try to recreate any of the specific moves?

2. Turn on some music and encourage the children to make up their own dances. They might like to hold scarves and see how they flow with them.

Things to Talk About

- Can you dance different ways to show different feelings?
- Can you pretend to be an animal while you dance?

This is a good activity to repeat another day.

A Play Celebration

Help your child learn to use words and practice making choices.

You'll Need

- A few different play options (art projects, blocks, toy cars, dress-up, etc.)

Directions

1. Let the children know of two or three different things they can choose to do—not everyone has to do the same thing.

2. Set everyone up with their different choice.

Remind the children that there are lots of ways to have fun.

Things to Talk About

- Do different people like doing different things?
- What do you like about the activity you chose?

Working out Problems

Help your child learn to solve problems through communication.

You'll Need

- One toy (doll, riding toy, ball, etc.)

Directions

1. Talk to the children about sharing. What do you do if everyone wants to play with the same toy?

2. Come up with some ideas. You might say "You can take a turn and then I'll get it back." Or if it's a toy like a ball, you can think of a game where you all use it together.

Things to Talk About

- Why is it good to talk when you're having a disagreement?

- Can you usually come up with a way to make everyone happy?

Name Tags

Help your child recognize and use symbols.

 Add a different shape to each child's card if they are very young.

You'll Need

- Index
- Markers

Things to Talk About

- Do you know what all the letters together are called?

- Do you want to sing the alphabet?

Directions

1. Make name tags for each child. Does each child know how to spell their name or, if they're younger, the first letter? Let each child see their name card before collecting them for later.

2. Later, set the name tags around a table and see if each child can find their name.

Let's Have a Parade

Help your child develop creative play and express feelings through music.

You'll Need

- Pie tins and wooden spoons for drums
- Paper towel rolls for horns
- Upbeat music
- Hats (optional)
- Flags (optional)

Directions

1. Hand out the pretend instruments, hats and flags (if you have them) and turn on some lively music. Let the children have a parade around the house or yard.

Explain that a parade is a celebration.

Things to Talk About

- Have you ever been to a parade?
- Why was it happening?

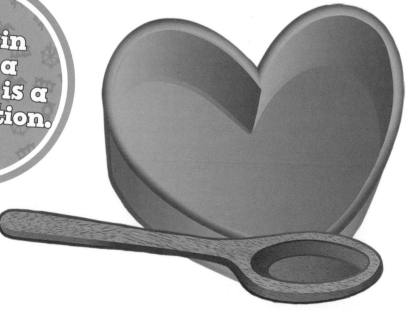

Birthday Parties

Help your child develop their imagination.

You'll Need

- Old party hats and favors
- Tape, string or ribbon
- Wrapping paper or newspaper to wrap pretend presents
- Modeling dough to make a pretend cake
- Cut straws for pretend candles
- Toy dishes
- Shoeboxes of toys to use as presents

Directions

1. Can the children tell you what a birthday party is like? Show the children the supplies you've gathered and see if they can think of how to use them for a pretend party.

2. Encourage the children to use the clay to make a cake, to wrap the presents, etc.

Things to Talk About

- What do you like about parties?
- Is there anything you don't like?

A Pretend School Bus

Help your child use play to work on feelings about new experiences.

You'll Need

- Chairs
- Schoolbooks, crayons, etc. (optional)
- Toy steering wheel or paper plate

Directions

1. Ask the children what they think it will be like to go to school. How do they think they will get there?

2. Have any of the children been on a school bus before? You can pretend by setting up rows of chairs while you pretend to be the driver.

3. Let the children act out waiting for the bus, getting on, sitting down, riding to school, etc.

Things to Talk About

- Do you think it will be fun to ride a school bus?
- What do you need to do when you're on the bus?

Simon Says

Help your child learn more about their body and learn to listen carefully.

You'll Need

- Nothing

Things to Talk About

- Do you have to listen carefully?
- Is it hard to do multiple things at once?

Directions

1. Acting as the leader, start a game of "Simon Says" with the children. Instead of trying to trick them, help them practice following directions by giving unusual instructions like "Touch your elbow on the floor" or "Pat your head and jump up and down."

End this game by singing "Head, Shoulders, Knees And Toes."

A Peaceful Solution

Help your child practice working cooperatively and taking turns.

You'll Need

- Jar with a narrow neck
- String
- Clothespins (not spring type)

Things to Talk About

- How can you get the clothespins out?
- Can you do it more easily by taking turns?

Directions

1. Tie a piece of string to each clothespin, making enough so there's one for each child. Place them all in the jar while leaving the string hanging out the top and over the side (3 or 4 at a time).

2. See if the children can pull out the clothespins. What happens if they all try to pull at the same time?

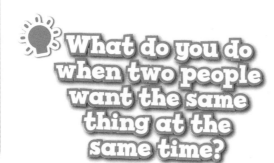 What do you do when two people want the same thing at the same time?

Make Some Changes

Help your children learn more about work and practice working together.

You'll Need

- Nothing

Things to Talk About

- Does cleaning up or making art create good changes?
- How do you feel when you've changed the way something looks for the better?

Directions

1. Can the children tell you how things they do change things? For example, picking up toys changes the way a room looks and eating their food changes how a plate looks.

2. Talk about the things you could do to make some changes today. They could rearrange a bookshelf, straighten up a playroom or, if the weather is nice, clean up a yard.

 A lot of people working together can make big changes.

Each One Is Separate

Help your child practice taking turns and working in a group.

You'll Need

- Nothing

Things to Talk About

- Is it difficult to hear the different voices?

- Do you think the song sounds a little different each time?

Directions

1. Talk about how everyone is unique and different, even when you're in a group. To help explain this, have everyone recite a nursery rhyme or sing a song together. Then take turns letting each child stay silent while everyone else sings. Can the quiet child hear the different voices?

2. Older children might like to play a game where they take turns saying the words to a rhyme or song. It might take some practice to get this right.

End this activity by singing a favorite song together.

A Pretend Wedding

Help your child develop creative play.

You'll Need

- Dress-up hats and scarves
- Fancy dress-up clothes (optional)
- Red or pink paper
- Small basket
- Small pillow
- Aluminum foil rings

Remind the children this is just a pretend wedding.

Directions

1. Have the children help you make a few props for a pretend wedding. Make paper rose petals by tearing small pieces of red or pink paper and rings out of aluminum foil. A scarf can be used as a veil.

2. Let the children put on a pretend wedding. If anyone doesn't want to participate, they can be a guest.

Things to Talk About

- Have you ever seen a wedding?
- Do you know anyone who is married?

Balance the Ring

Help your child develop coordination and the ability to keep trying.

You'll Need

- Aluminum foil rings
- Small pillow or folded towel

Things to Talk About

- Is is difficult to balance the rings?
- Does it get easier the more you practice?

Directions

1. Have any of the children been to a wedding? Was there a ring bearer? Can they show you how the ring bearer carries the rings?

2. Make two rings out of aluminum foil and place them on a small pillow or a small folded towel. Let each child take a turn pretending to be a ring bearer. Can they walk from one side of the room to the other without dropping the rings?

Make larger foil crowns for the children to balance on their heads.

Jump Over

Help your child learn to keep trying and improve their coordination.

You'll Need

- Masking tape
- Jump rope

Directions

1. Have the children warm up by stretching as high as they can, jumping up and down and touching their toes.

2. See if the children can jump over a rope without touching it. If they're older, have the other children hold the rope an inch or two off the floor. Or you can place two pieces of masking tape on the ground and see if the children can jump far enough to clear both of them.

Things to Talk About

- How far do you think you can jump?
- Do you think you'll be able to jump farther when you're older?

Remind the children that everyone's good at something.

Treasure Hunt

Help your child develop their curiosity and learn to look carefully.

You'll Need

- Paper
- Pencil

Directions

1. Prepare secret messages using the pencil and paper, and hide them around the house for the children to find. Each message should give a clue about where to find the next one.

2. If the children are older, you can write the clues in the form of a riddle. Have the children work together to figure out each new clue.

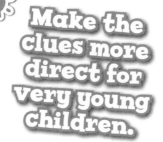

Make the clues more direct for very young children.

Things to Talk About

- Are riddles fun to figure out?
- Is it easier when you talk about them with other people?

Kickball

Help your child learn about playing on a team.

You'll Need

- Ball sturdy enough for kicking

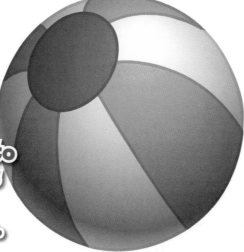

You might want to have a few balls if playing with younger children.

Directions

1. Explain to the children that when people kick a ball, they might accidentally knock something over or break it. If you're going to play a game with a ball, you need a safe space to do so.

2. Go outside for this game and divide the children into two teams. Encourage them to kick the ball back and forth to one another, letting each teammate take a turn.

Things to Talk About

- Have you ever wanted to be on a team?
- What kind of team would you like to be on?

Shoe Match

Help your child learn to recognize likeness and difference.

You'll Need

- The children's shoes
- 2 boxes or baskets

Directions

1. Start this game by placing one shoe from each pair in one basket and the second shoe in the other.

2. One at a time, let the children take turns selecting a shoe from one container and then trying to find its match in the other one. Replace the shoes each time to make sure the game is equally challenging for each child.

Things to Talk About

- What do all the shoes have in common?
- How are they different?

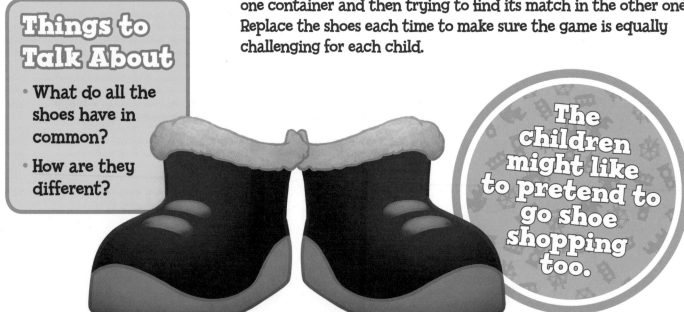

The children might like to pretend to go shoe shopping too.

Bowling

Help your child develop their coordination and practice taking turns.

You'll Need

- Empty plastic soda or water bottles
- Plastic ball or sock ball
- Masking tape

 Older children might like to keep score.

Directions

1. Help the children set up the bottles as pins. Arrange them in a triangle like real bowling pins.

2. Put a piece of tape on the floor to show the children where to stand before rolling the ball toward the pins. Let them take turns "bowling" and resetting the pins.

Things to Talk About

- Do you have fun, even when you don't knock down all the pins?
- Does your aim improve the more you practice?

It doesn't really matter what we do, a friend just wants to play with you!

Cooking Together

Discover where food comes from and the importance of trying new foods, as well as some science skills!.

A Party Cake

Help your child practice working cooperatively and learn more about foods.

You'll Need

- Your favorite cake recipe and ingredients
- Measuring cups and spoons
- Mixing bowls and mixing spoons
- Cake or cupcake pans

Directions

1. Start by talking to your child about how a cake is made and make a list of all the jobs that must be done, including washing hands, measuring ingredients, mixing them together, greasing the pans, beating eggs and cleaning up.

2. Follow your favorite recipe to bake a cake, letting your child help when possible.

Things to Talk About

- Why is it important that we follow the recipe?
- Can you read the numbers on the measuring cups and spoons?

If doing this with more than one child, decide which job each one gets to do from the list you made.

Instant Pudding

Help your child practice taking turns and waiting.

It's OK to overshake to make sure that each child gets the same number of turns.

You'll Need

- Instant pudding mix
- Milk
- Jar or plastic container with a tight-fitting lid
- Measuring cup
- Cups and spoons

Things to Talk About

- Do you like taking turns?
- What can we do while we're waiting for the pudding to be ready?

Directions

1. Open the instant pudding mix and help your child pour it into a jar. Pour in the amount of milk called for on the box directions.

2. Tightly screw on the lid. Let your child shake the jar for 15 seconds, taking turns with other children (or with you, if doing this activity with just one child). The pudding needs to be shaken for about 2 minutes, or eight turns.

3. When the shaking is done, pour the pudding into the cups and let it sit in the refrigerator for at least 5 minutes before eating.

Making Applesauce

Help your child learn how to follow directions and practice making choices.

You'll Need

- 4 apples
- Water
- ¼ cup sugar or honey
- Pan
- Mixing spoon
- Cinnamon
- Measuring cups and spoons

Directions

1. Have your child help you wash and dry the apples. Peel the apples and let your child help you slice them into chunks, if they can, with a plastic knife.

2. Put the apples in a pan. Add ½ cup water and simmer the apples over medium heat for 15 minutes.

3. Stir in the sugar or honey and a sprinkle of cinnamon. Serve warm or cold.

Things to Talk About

- Do you know where apples come from?
- Is it more fun to buy applesauce at the store or make it at home?

Explain that there are some parts of cooking that are only safe for grown-ups to do.

Thumbprint Pies

Help your child learn how to work cooperatively in the kitchen.

You'll Need

- 1 cup flour
- ½ tsp salt
- 4 Tbsp butter
- 2 Tbsp water
- Mixing bowl
- Cookie sheet
- Mixing spoon or fork
- Jam

Directions

1. Let your child help you measure the flour, salt, butter and water in a bowl. Take turns mixing the dough until it is smooth.

2. Let your child play with the dough, then show them how to roll it into a small ball. Put the dough balls on a cookie sheet and let your child mash their thumbprint into each one. Bake at 350 degrees F for 8 to 10 minutes. Once cooled, you can add a small amount of jam to each thumbprint.

Save leftover pies in an airtight container in the refrigerator.

Things to Talk About

- Do you like working with the dough?
- What can we do while waiting for the pies to bake?

Making Butter

Help your child learn how food is made and how to wait patiently.

You'll Need

- 1 pint heavy cream
- Container with tight-fitting lid
- Salt
- Spoon
- Butter knife
- Crackers or bread

Things to Talk About

- What can we do while waiting for the lumps to form?
- Do you want to sing a song or make up a story?

Directions

1. Pour the pint of heavy cream into the jar and tightly close the lid. Take turns shaking the jar with your child. It can take 10 to 20 minutes of shaking for the cream to become lumpy.

2. Once the cream forms large lumps, pour off the liquid (or drain it through a cheesecloth) and add a pinch of salt before giving the lumps a good stir. Let your child spread a little bit of butter on crackers or bread for a snack.

You can also challenge your child to be as quiet as they can for a short while.

Making Peanut Butter

Help your child learn how store-bought foods can be made at home.

If you don't have a food processor, crush the peanuts as finely as you can and add just enough oil to make a paste.

You'll Need

- ⅓ cup shelled peanuts, dry-roasted
- Wooden spoon or mallet
- Rolling pin
- Plastic food storage bag
- Food processor
- Crackers
- Butter knife

Directions

1. Pour the roasted peanuts into a plastic food storage bag. Take turns pounding and crushing the peanuts with a wooden spoon or mallet.

2. Once the peanut pieces are fairly small, let your child finish crushing them with a rolling pin. Pour the crushed peanuts into a food processor and blend until creamy. Let your child put a small amount of the peanut butter on crackers for a snack.

Things to Talk About

- Did you like crushing the peanuts?
- Do you think the peanut butter you buy at a store is made the same way?

Instant Oatmeal

Help your child develop a healthy curiosity about food.

You'll Need

- Instant oatmeal packet (or any instant hot cereal or even hot chocolate)
- Hot water
- Bowls
- Spoons
- Cinnamon

Directions

1. Let your child pour the oatmeal in their bowl while the water is heating. Add the hot water yourself, pouring it carefully. Let your child mix the two together with a spoon until it cools. Add a sprinkle of cinnamon if you'd like.

 Your child might like to see a video of an astronaut eating similar "instant" food.

Things to Talk About

- Why do we need to add hot water to the food?
- Do you think it would work as well with cold water?

Egg Salad Sandwiches

Help your child learn more about foods.

You'll Need

- Eggs (1 per person)
- Saucepan
- Mixing bowl
- Fork or potato masher
- Mayonnaise
- Bread
- Crayons (optional)

Directions

1. If you'd like, let your child (and any person making an egg) mark their initials on the shell of one egg with a crayon.

2. Place the eggs in a pan full of cold water. Bring the pan to a boil over medium-high heat, then cover, remove from heat and set aside for 10 minutes. Drain the eggs and cool them in ice water.

3. Help your child peel their egg and any others. Take turns mashing the peeled eggs in a bowl. Mix in mayonnaise to taste, then let your child make their own sandwich.

Things to Talk About

- What happened to the egg when you boiled it?
- Do you like making your own sandwich?

Pack up the sandwiches to take on a picnic lunch.

Dad Tiger's Concoction

Help your child learn more about foods.

You can also use blueberries, blackberries or raspberries.

You'll Need

- 2 cups fresh strawberries (or 12-ounce bag frozen berries)
- Banana
- ½ cup wheat germ, rolled oats or flax seed
- 1 cup milk
- Bowl
- Potato masher or fork
- Butter knife
- Blender
- Cups

Directions

1. Let the strawberries thaw, if frozen, and place them in a bowl. Let your child mash them using a potato masher or fork.

2. If your child is old enough, let them cut up the banana into slices.

3. Put the fruit in a blender and purée it, adding the wheat germ and milk a little at a time. Once everything is incorporated and smooth, serve the smoothie in cups.

Things to Talk About

- Do you know what a "concoction" is?
- Do you like your fruit concoction?

Fruit Salad

Help your child learn more about foods and recognize likeness and difference.

You'll Need

- Bowl
- 3 or 4 kinds of fruits (banana, apple, orange, pear, pineapple, grapes, melon, strawberries, etc.)
- Knife
- Small cups or bowls
- Spoons

Directions

1. Let your child help you wash and dry the fruit. While you do any necessary cutting or slicing, your child can help:
- Peel oranges or bananas
- Separate orange pieces
- Mix the fruit
- Put the salad into cups

2. Once the fruit salad is made, talk about the fruits. How are they different from one another?

Things to Talk About

- Is each fruit soft or crunchy?
- Are the colors the same?
- Do any taste sweet?

Close your eyes and guess each fruit as you eat.

Egg Drop Soup

Help your child learn more about how cooking changes ingredients.

You'll Need

- Chicken or vegetable broth
- Egg
- Saucepan
- Spoon
- Bowl
- Fork

Things to Talk About

- What did the egg look like when we first cracked it open?
- What happened to the egg in the hot broth?

Let your child stand on a step stool (or be held by another adult) to see how the egg cooks.

Directions

1. Heat the broth in a saucepan until it's boiling.

2. Meanwhile, let your child watch as you crack an egg in a bowl and then mix it with a fork. Once it's fully mixed, your child might like to stir it for a bit too.

3. Stir the boiling broth and slowly pour in the egg. Once the egg is cooked, serve the soup.

Pancakes or Waffles

Let your child pretend to cook while you make the pancakes or waffles.

Help your child learn more about foods and try out different roles.

You'll Need

- Skillet or waffle iron
- Your favorite pancake or waffle recipe
- Spatula
- Bowl
- Measuring cups and spoons
- Mixing spoon
- Syrup or honey

Directions

1. Prepare pancakes or waffles according to your favorite recipe. Let your child help as much as they can. Children can do things like:
   - Beating eggs
   - Adding flour
   - Mixing ingredients
   - Setting the table

Things to Talk About

- What happens to the batter when we heat it up?
- Do you have a favorite topping for pancakes or waffles?

263

Making Pizza

Help your child learn more about foods and practice waiting.

Make this easier by making pizza on bagels or English muffins.

You'll Need

- 1 packet yeast
- 1¼ cups warm water
- 3½–4 cups flour
- Tomato sauce
- Grated mozzarella cheese
- Bowl
- Mixing spoon
- Cookie sheet

Directions

1. Prepare the dough by mixing together the yeast and warm water. Stir in half the flour until smooth, then stir in the rest of the flour and knead until dough forms. Let the dough rise in a bowl for 30 minutes, then knead again.

2. Preheat the oven to 425 degrees F. Give your child a small piece of dough to play with and flatten to make their own personal pizza. Let your child spoon on some tomato sauce and top their pizza with cheese, then bake on a greased cookie sheet in the oven for 20 minutes.

Things to Talk About

- What can we do while the dough is rising?
- What else could we put on a pizza?

Making Tacos

Help your child learn more about foods and making choices.

You'll Need

- Corn tortillas or taco shells
- Ground meat and/or black beans
- Taco seasoning
- Lettuce
- Tomatoes
- Shredded cheese
- Green pepper
- Salsa (optional)

Directions

1. Brown the ground meat (and/or warm the black beans) in a skillet and add taco seasoning. Cut the tomatoes and peppers while your child tears the lettuce. Your child could also put the prepared vegetables and cheese in bowls.

2. Let your child prepare their own taco by filling tortillas or taco shells with their favorite ingredients.

Make the salsa on page 275 for this recipe.

Things to Talk About

- Do you like crispy shells or soft tortillas?
- Do you like making your own tacos?

Cookie Decorating

Help your child practice taking turns and sharing.

You'll Need

- Your favorite cookie recipe
- Rolling pin
- Cookie-cutters or plastic knife
- Cookie decorations (sprinkles, chocolate chips, cinnamon sugar)

Serve the cookies as a special snack or dessert.

Directions

1. Let your child help you make your favorite cookie dough by helping measure and mix the ingredients. Your child might like to roll the dough into balls to make their own cookies.

2. Let your child decorate a few cookies. They could make thumbprints, cut the dough into special shapes or add edible decorations like sprinkles. Bake as directed in your recipe.

Things to Talk About

- Did you enjoy mixing the dough and decorating the cookies?
- Do you want to share the cookies with anyone?

Making Bread

Help your child learn more about how foods are made and practice waiting.

You'll Need

- 3 cups flour
- 2 tsp salt
- ¾ tsp active dry yeast
- 1½ cups lukewarm water
- Parchment paper
- Dutch oven or oven-safe pot with lid

Directions

1. Let your child help measure the ingredients and mix them all together in a large bowl. Cover the bowl with a dish towel and let the dough rise for 6 to 8 hours or overnight.

2. Turn the dough out onto floured parchment paper, folding it over onto itself at least once. Shape the dough into a ball and cover with a dish towel, letting it rise for at least one more hour.

3. Preheat the oven, Dutch oven and lid to 450 degrees F. Once hot, remove the Dutch oven and carefully place the parchment paper with the dough ball inside. Cover with the hot lid and bake covered for 30 minutes, then uncovered for 15 minutes. Let the bread cool for at least 10 minutes before you slice.

Things to Talk About

- What did the dough look like before and after it rose?
- How is this bread different from bread we buy at the store?

Making Sandwiches

Help your child practice making choices and learn more about foods.

You'll Need

- Bread
- Cheese slices
- Filling, such as lunch meat, egg salad or tuna salad
- Lettuce leaves
- Mayonnaise or mustard
- Butter knife

Things to Talk About

- What is your favorite thing to put on a sandwich?
- Do you always choose the same filling?

Remind your child to wash their hands before touching food.

Directions

1. Have your child help you arrange the sandwich ingredients on plates or platters. Help your child make their own choices and their own sandwich.

2. Eat the sandwiches right away or wrap them up and save them for later, maybe for a picnic.

Graham Cracker Treats

Help your child learn more about preparing different foods.

You'll Need

- Graham crackers
- 1 cup peanut butter
- ¼ cup honey
- ½ cup nonfat dry milk
- Rolling pin
- Bowl
- Food storage bag

Things to Talk About

- Do you like playing with the dough?
- How is it different from modeling dough?

Use any kind of nut butter you'd like.

Directions

1. Put two or three graham crackers into a food storage bag and let your child use the rolling pin to crush them. Repeat as necessary until you have a full cup of cracker crumbs.

2. Mix the cracker crumbs, peanut butter, honey and dry milk together until a dough forms. Show your child how to roll the dough into small balls. Refrigerate the balls for 30 minutes to make them firm. Then they're ready to eat!

Milkshakes

Help your child learn more about food and work.

You'll Need

- Ice cream
- Scoop or spoon
- Milk
- Jar or plastic container with a tight-fitting lid
- Cups
- Straws (optional)

Directions

1. Let your child help you scoop ice cream into a large container. (About four large scoops in a 1-quart jar works well.) Add milk until the jar is nearly full, then close the lid tightly.

2. Take turns shaking the milk and ice cream until the lumps are dissolved. Pour the shake into cups and drink with straws, if you'd like.

Take turns counting to 10 together as each person shakes the jar.

Things to Talk About

- What work did you have to do to make the milkshake?
- Is there an easier way to get a milkshake?

Dried Apple Rings

Help your child learn more about food and practice waiting.

You'll Need

- Cookie sheet
- 3 or 4 apples
- Knife
- Apple corer (optional)
- Vegetable oil
- Paper towel

Let your child check the apples' progress by turning on the oven light.

Directions

1. While you core and slice the apples into ¼-inch slices, let your child grease a cookie sheet with vegetable oil and a paper towel.

2. When you're finished slicing, let your child arrange the apple slices on the cookie sheet. Drying the apples takes 6 to 8 hours in an oven in the lowest possible setting.

Things to Talk About

- What can you do while you wait for the apples to dry?
- How can you measure that amount of time?

Granola Gifts

Help your child learn more about food and practice sharing.

Remind your child that you are fortunate to be able to share food with others.

You'll Need

- Plain packaged granola
- Raisins
- Chopped dried fruit
- Sesame seeds
- Chopped nuts
- Bowls
- Spoons
- Small plastic bags
- Ribbon or yarn
- Paper
- Tape

Directions

1. Let your child mix up their own batch of granola in a small bowl, adding a spoonful of each ingredient of their choosing. Once the mixing is done, they can spoon it into a plastic bag.

2. Help your child tie yarn or ribbon around the bag to close it and make a festive package. Can your child think of someone who would enjoy receiving a granola gift? Help them write their name on a piece of paper to tape to the bag.

Things to Talk About

- How does it feel to give a gift to someone?
- How many granola gifts could we make?

269

Baker Aker's Nutritious Snack

Help your child learn more about trying new foods.

You'll Need

- ¾ cup nonfat dry milk
- 1 cup peanut butter
- 1 Tbsp butter
- Chopped nuts
- Raisins
- Dates (optional)
- Graham cracker crumbs (optional)
- Bowl
- Spoon

Directions

1. Let your child taste each ingredient before combining them to make Baker Aker's nutritious snack.

2. Combine the butter and peanut butter, then add the nonfat dry milk and mix thoroughly. Add nuts, raisins and dates as desired.

3. Let your child help you shape the mixture into balls and roll each one in cracker crumbs, if desired.

Remind your child to try new food because it might taste good.

Things to Talk About

- Were there any foods you didn't like?
- Do you think you might like that food some day?

Vegetable Soup

Ask your child to name other healthy foods they like to eat.

Help your child learn more about food and understand the difference between real and pretend.

You'll Need

- Vegetable soup (homemade or canned)

Things to Talk About

- Where does vegetable soup come from?
- What would happen if you planted a can of vegetable soup?

Directions

1. Begin this activity by talking about how vegetables grow. Has your child ever seen a vegetable plant?

2. Serve some vegetable soup for lunch or a snack. Can your child name the vegetables in the soup?

Homemade Noodles

Help your child learn more about how different foods are made.

You'll Need

- 2 cups flour
- Egg
- ⅓ cup water
- Bowl
- Large pan
- Chicken or vegetable broth
- Carrots, onion, celery, potatoes (optional)
- Plastic knife

Directions

1. In a large bowl, combine the flour, egg and water. Your child can help mix the ingredients and knead the dough into a smooth ball. Let your child roll out a piece of dough and use the plastic knife to cut strips of noodles to add to boiling broth, when you're ready.

2. If you want to add chopped onion, celery, carrots or potatoes to the broth, cook them before adding the noodles. The noodles will cook in 2 minutes once added to boiling broth.

Things to Talk About

- How do these taste different from boxed noodles?
- Are all the noodles exactly the same?

Arroz Con Leche

Help your child learn more about preparing different kinds of food.

You'll Need

- ½ cup rice
- Cinnamon sticks
- Raisins
- Orange peel
- 1 large can evaporated milk
- ½ can condensed milk
- Vanilla extract
- Saucepan
- Spoon
- Small bowls

Directions

1. Boil the rice according to package instructions, adding the cinnamon stick and orange peel to the water with the rice. Remove the peel and sticks once the rice is cooked.

2. Let your child help you combine the rice, evaporated milk and condensed milk in a saucepan. Add a dash of vanilla and let your child stir the mixture. Cook the ingredients on a stove over medium heat until it reaches a pudding-like consistency. Stir in raisins, if desired. Let the mixture cool slightly before serving.

Any chopped or dried fruit can be used in place of raisins.

Things to Talk About

- Have you ever had rice pudding?
- What else would you add to it?

Peanut Butter and Fruit

Help your child learn more about choosing healthy snacks.

You'll Need

- Peanut butter
- Butter knives
- Fruit (apples, bananas, pears)
- Crackers

Make your own peanut butter (page 259) if you'd like.

Directions

1. Let your child closely inspect the fruit as you wash it. How does it look? Feel? Smell?

2. Let your child watch as you slice the fruit, then show them how to spread peanut butter on the fruit and apples as a snack.

Things to Talk About

- Which fruit do you like best with peanut butter?
- What are some other ways you like to eat fruit?

Gingerbread Faces

Help your child learn to talk about feelings.

You'll Need

- Mirror
- Your favorite gingerbread recipe and ingredients
- Bowls, mixing spoons, cookie sheets
- Measuring cups and spoons
- Icing

Directions

1. Ask your child if they can think of a time when they felt happy. What about sad or bored? Encourage them to show you how their face looks when they feel this way. Let them see their own expression in a mirror.

2. Have your child help you make gingerbread cookies that show different expressions. Use the icing to draw happy, sad, angry and bored faces.

Things to Talk About

- Can you always tell how a person is feeling by the way they look?

Popcorn

Help your child learn more about how cooking changes different foods.

You'll Need

- ⅓ cup popcorn kernels
- Oil
- Heavy pan with lid
- Bowls

Directions

1. Show your child some popcorn kernels and ask if they know what happens when the popcorn is heated.

2. Add a thin coat of oil to the bottom of a pan and heat it over medium high. Add a few kernels to the pan. Once they pop, remove them and add the rest of the kernels in an even layer. Cover the pan, leaving the lid slightly ajar, and gently shake the pan as the kernels begins to pop. Remove the pan from the heat once the popping slows and serve.

Things to Talk About

- Why did we cover the pan when popping the kernels?
- Do you want to pretend to be a popping kernel?

You can also pop the kernels in the microwave in a paper bag.

Salsa and Tortilla Chips

Help your child develop cooking skills and learn more about their world.

You'll Need

- 1 cup finely chopped tomatoes
- ½ Tbsp finely chopped green peppers
- 1 Tbsp lime juice
- 2 Tbsp water
- ½ Tbsp finely chopped onion
- Bowl
- Spoon
- Tortilla chips, crackers or pita bread
- Serving plate

Directions

1. Let your child help you measure and mix the ingredients early in the day. Let the mixture sit for a while before serving.

2. Enjoy the salsa and chips at lunch or for a snack later in the day.

Add salt, pepper and minced garlic if you'd like.

Things to Talk About

- How do you think tortilla chips are made?
- Is there anything else you think would taste good with salsa?

We gotta try new food because it might taste good!

♫ Clean Up, Pick Up, Put Away ♫

Clean up, pick up, put away
Clean up every day

Uh oh, O, this bedroom is a mess!
Now let's clean it up.
Clean up

Clean up, pick up, put away
Clean up every day
Clean up, pick up, put away
Clean up every day

Pick up your toys off the floor,
And put them in your special drawer.
Pick up

Clean up, pick up, put away
Clean up every day
Clean up, pick up, put away
Clean up every day

Where does this go? Let's take a look.
There! And put away our favorite book.
Put away

Clean up, pick up, put away
Clean up every day
Clean up, pick up, put away
Clean up every day

♪ Count Down To Calm Down ♪

Close your eyes and lie in bed,
And let's count down to calm down.
Five, four, three, two, one.

The moon shines a bright light.
It's time to start dreaming and sleep
  for the night.
You can dream you're counting stars,
Or bouncing off the puffy clouds,
Or sleeping on the moon.

It's time to sleep, the day is done.
Let's count down to calm down.
Five, four, three, two, one.

♪ Find a Way to Play Together ♪

When we want to play in our
own special way,
We sometimes forget about
our friends.
If we want to play house,
Be a dinosaur, or a mouse,
Together is the best way to pretend.

Find a way to play together
And find a way to share with
each other.
Playing is great,
Playing together is so much better.
Find a way to play together!

Each one of us brings our own
special gifts,
That makes us who we are.
And when we play together, the time

we spend is better,
And more exciting by far!

Find a way to play together,
And find a way to care for
each other.
Playing is great,
Playing together is even better.
Find a way to play together!

🎵 Keep Trying 🎵

When you can't do something new,
Keep trying and trying
Till it works for you,
Before you know it, I think you'll find,
Practice makes you better all the time.

Try, try, try, try, try it again
Try, try, try, try, try it again

Keep trying, you'll get better.
Try, try, try

When you're trying to do
a brand new thing,
Don't give up if it's not working
It'll get easier every time you try,
Practice makes you better all the time.

Try, try, try, try, try it again
Try, try, try, try, try it again

Keep trying, you'll get better.
Try, try, try
Keep trying, you'll get better.
Try, try, try

♪ Everyone Is Big Enough ♪ To Do Something

Everyone is big enough,
Big enough to do something!

You can help build a playhouse
by getting my tools.
I can reach in spaces that are
too small for you.
You can choose the color and
paint half the door.
If you pick me up I can paint
higher than before.

Everyone is big enough,
Big enough to do something!

You can help me bake a cake
by mixing up the batter.
If you have a spill, I can help
clean up the splatter.
You can help water the flowers
with the hose.
I can put away the dishes,
just show me where they go.
Everyone is big enough,
Big enough to do something!
Everyone is big enough,
Big enough to do something!

Find Your Own Way To Say I Love You

Find your own way to say I love you.

Spending time with you is one way
to say that I love you.
We can look at clouds or sing out loud.
It doesn't matter what we do.
Say it by playing music with you
And having fun with you too.

There are different ways
to say I love you.

Helping someone is one way
to say that I love you.
We can learn to dance or skate hand
in hand to say I love you.
Making you some art or we could
explore the stars.
There are so many ways
to say I love you.

When You Wait, You Can Play, Sing Or Imagine Anything

When you wait,
You can play, sing
or imagine anything!

You can sing a silly song,
Get your friends to sing along,
Play with your toys,
Something you enjoy,
Play a card game,
Or a guessing game.
So many ways to make the
waiting go away.

When you wait,
You can play, sing
or imagine anything!
[x2]

Use your imagination,
then you'll see.
Pretend to be anyone you want
to be.
Pretend you are a fish swimming
in the sea,
Or a dinosaur peeking over the
tree.

When you wait,
You can play, sing
or imagine anything!
[x2]

♪ Stop, Think ♪ And Choose!

It's time to make a choice,
I don't know what to do.
I'll stop, think and choose.
Stop, think and choose!
Stop, think and choose!

What do I eat in the morning?
I'll think clues and then I'll choose.
I'll choose blueberries.
Stop, think and choose!
Stop, think and choose!

One thing I have to choose
Is what game I like to play.
I'll choose to play ball all day.

Stop, think and choose!
Stop, think and choose!
Stop, think and choose!
Stop, think and choose!

Media Lab Books
For inquiries, call 646-838-6637

Copyright 2019 Topix Media Lab

Published by Topix Media Lab
14 Wall Street, Suite 4B
New York, NY 10005

Printed in China

ISBN-13: 978-1-948174-16-9
ISBN-10: 1-948174-16-2

With many thanks to Julia Travers, for her unwavering dedication to children's education.

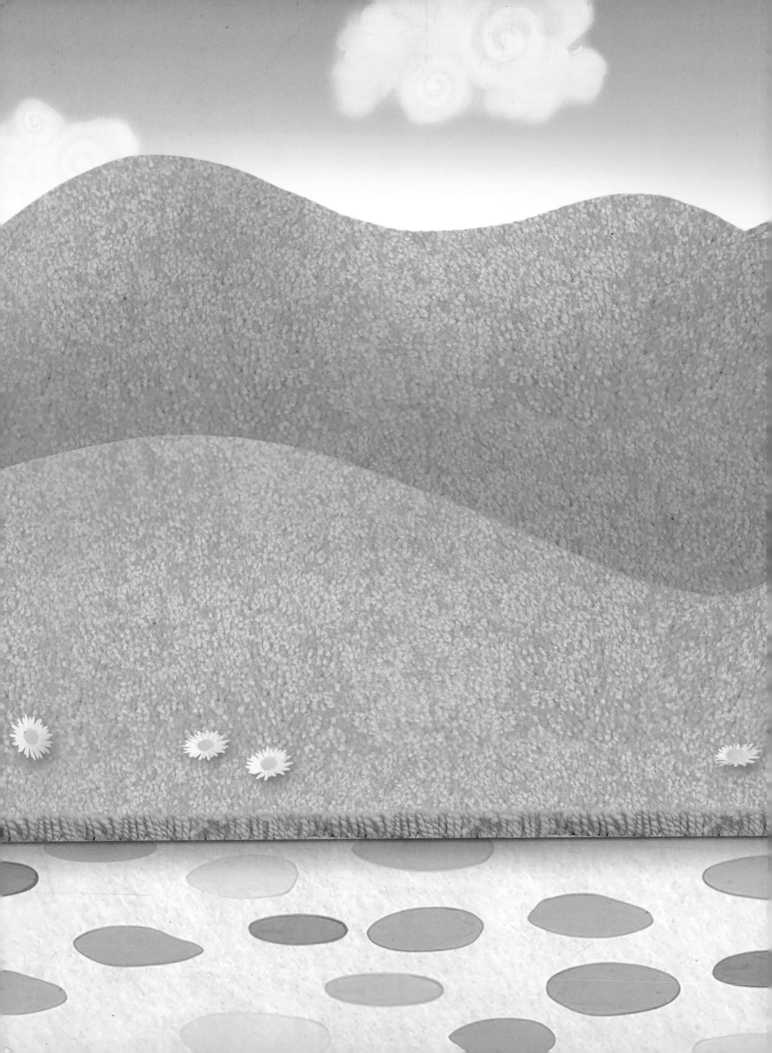